DEVOTIONS®

I walk in the way of righteousness, along the paths of justice.

— *Proverbs 8:20*

Gary Allen, Editor | **Margaret Williams,** Project Editor | Photo by Jupiterimages/Comstock/Thinkstock®

DEVOTIONS® is published quarterly by Standard Publishing, Cincinnati, Ohio, www.standardpub.com. © 2011 by Standard Publishing. All rights reserved. Topics based on the Home Daily Bible Readings, International Sunday School Lessons. © 2008 by the Committee on the Uniform Series. Printed in the U.S.A. All Scripture quotations, unless otherwise indicated, are taken from the *HOLY BIBLE, NEW INTERNATIONAL VERSION®. NIV®.* Copyright © 1973, 1978, 1984 by Biblical Inc.™ Used by permission of Zondervan. All rights reserved. Where noted, Scripture quotations are from the following, used with permission of the copyright holders, all rights reserved: The *Revised Standard Version of the Bible (RSV),* copyrighted 1946, 1952, © 1971, 1973. The *Contemporary English Version (CEV)* copyright © 1991, 1992, 1995 by American Bible Society.

Little Ol' Me

What is man that you are mindful of him, the son of man that you care for him? (Psalm 8:4).

Scripture: Psalm 8
Song: "Holy Father, Great Creator"

I feel insignificant when I remember that I'm only one person in a world of nearly 7 billion human beings. I also feel insignificant when I look at a starry sky. According to CNN.com, astronomers have estimated that many million more stars exist in the universe than the 70 sextillion visible through telescopes.

I think I know how David felt when he gazed at the heavens. It boggles the senses to consider that the almighty Creator thinks about little ol' me and actually *cares* for me. But He does.

God sent His Son to die for me, and daily He watches over me. He provides everything I need for today and promises He will never leave me or forsake me in the future (Hebrews 13:5).

Recently, my wife and I rode the cog railway to the top of Pikes Peak. At 14,110 feet we had a commanding view of lower mountaintops in every direction, and we saw prairies stretching for many miles to the east. Two songs flooded my mind: "How Great Thou Art" and "He's Got the Whole World in His Hands." We can be so grateful He's great, so thankful that He keeps us in His hands.

Father, I thank You for creating a world of vast beauty, order, and delight. I sometimes feel insignificant in this universe, but I know You love me. In Jesus' name I pray. Amen.

March 1–4. **Jim Dyet** is a retired minister and editor. He and his wife, Gloria, have been married 52 years and reside in Colorado Springs. They have three adult children and two granddaughters.

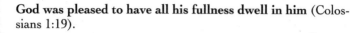

More Than a Superhero

God was pleased to have all his fullness dwell in him (Colossians 1:19).

Scripture: Colossians 1:15-19
Song: "Fairest Lord Jesus"

When I was a kid, I enjoyed reading superhero comic books. Endowed with superhuman qualities, Captain Marvel, the Green Lantern, and Superman transported me into a fantasy land. If only I had kept a few of those early comic books to sell today! In February 2010, an original 1938 Superman Action Comics #1 was sold at auction for $10 million. I wonder whether the buyer keeps a load of diamonds, gold, and kryptonite in a well-locked safe.

Although the concept of superheroes appeals to children, and even to a number of adults, we must never perceive Jesus as simply a superhero. He is a real person, and He is the Son of God. As Paul informed the Colossians, Jesus is preeminent. No one can compare with Him. He is the source of everything that exists, and He sustains the universe. Furthermore, He is the head of the church, and He shares God's essential nature and characteristics.

Years ago, I put aside my comic books and childish fascination with powerful superheroes and started reading God's book every day. I may never be offered $10 million for my Bible, but it is worth far more than that to me because it features Jesus.

Father, I am grateful that Your Son is in control of the universe and is the head of the church. I can trust Him to hold my life together when the winds of adversity strike, and I know He will guide me all the days of my life. In His name I pray. Amen.

A Full-Body Makeover

Not only so, but we ourselves, who have the firstfruits of the Spirit, groan inwardly as we wait eagerly for our adoption as sons, the redemption of our bodies (Romans 8:23).

Scripture: Romans 8:18-25
Song: "When the Roll Is Called Up Yonder"

At age 40, John was almost totally bald. Just one hair stood like a sentinel guarding his scalp. Not wanting to lose that single hair, John patted it and lavished hair cream on it daily. However, one fateful morning he looked into the bathroom mirror and saw that the last, lone hair had deserted its post. Horrified, he cried out: "I'm bald. I'm bald!"

I have heard it said that aging is not for sissies, and I agree. My list of aches, pains, and ailments is growing as I age. So is my list of doctors: primary care physician, ophthalmologist, cardiologist, dermatologist, urologist, and otolaryngologist. My list of prescription pills is growing too. As for baldness—the top of my head used to resemble the waves of an ocean, but the waves disappeared long ago; now only the beach remains.

But as I age, I increasingly anticipate my resurrection body. It will be like Jesus' glorified body (see Philippians 3:20, 21): free of pain and weakness and incapable of dying. Perhaps I will even have a full head of hair again.

The prospect of resurrection can fill us with hope and prompt us to sing a doxology instead of a dirge. The best is yet to be!

Father, help me deal triumphantly with the effects of aging. I thank You that Your grace is sufficient for me, and I look forward to receiving a glorified body some day. In the meantime, may I live with peace and joy. Through Christ I pray. Amen.

 **Are We Really Listening?**

Listen to my instruction and be wise; do not ignore it (Proverbs 8:33).

Scripture: Proverbs 8:22-35
Song: "Speak, My Lord"

A cartoon shows a man seated in a recliner and reading a newspaper. His wife exclaims, "George, the garage is on fire!" He replies, "That's nice, Dear."

Many married couples can relate to the cartoon's message: Husbands can be very poor listeners. Of course, there is always the possibility a husband is losing his sense of hearing. In that case a simple test can determine whether hearing aids might improve his quality of life—and his wife's.

Good hearing and good listening aren't necessarily synonymous. A person may hear every word a nutritionist speaks about healthful eating—and then enter the nearest restaurant and order pecan pie with two scoops of ice cream. Another person may hear her doctor say she must exercise at least 30 minutes daily or risk a heart attack, but she may continue to play the role of a couch potato. In each case neither person actually *listened*.

Wisdom is personified in Jesus and disclosed in Scripture. If we merely read Jesus' words and dismiss them, we have only heard them. But if we read and obey His words, we have listened to them. Let's be like the boy Samuel, who prayed, "Speak, Lord, for your servant is listening" (see 1 Samuel 3:10).

O Lord, I need wisdom so that I may make good decisions, do the right thing, and honor You. Incline my heart to Your Word, and teach me the importance of truly listening as You speak. In Christ I pray. Amen.

Hebrew Honey

That same night they are to eat the meat roasted over the fire, along with bitter herbs, and bread made without yeast (Exodus 12:8).

Scripture: Exodus 12:1-8
Song: "He Keeps Me Singing"

My husband and I were invited to share a Passover meal with friends. As we gathered to eat, I asked the hostess to tell me about the pretty green salad sitting next to some roasted lamb and unleavened bread. She explained that it represented bitter herbs and contained ground horseradish and lettuce.

Hmmm. That didn't sound very appetizing. But then I remembered that the bitter herbs were to represent the bitterness of slavery, so I decided to eat one serving. As we sat down to eat, I took a generous forkful of the "herbs" and put it in my mouth. I could barely choke it down! Quickly, I took a bite of the unleavened bread. It was sweet with honey. Suddenly the herbs did not taste as bitter; they had been swallowed up in the sweetness of the honeyed bread.

Jesus declares that He is the "bread of life" (John 6:35). How true! He is our sustenance and our sweetness, making the bitterness of life bearable.

Father God, before the bitter times of life become unbearable, please remind me to feast on the "bread of life," both for strength and for comfort. Thank You, Father. In the name of Jesus, who lives and reigns with You and the Holy Spirit, one God, now and forever, amen.

March 5–11. **Brenda J. Garver** is a writer living in Farwell, Michigan, who loves to read and collect old books. She and her husband have three grown children and a new grandson.

Wonder at Any Age

Great are the works of the LORD; they are pondered by all who delight in them (Psalm 111:2).

Scripture: Psalm 111
Song: "How Great Thou Art"

Children aren't the only ones who can have a sense of wonder. Middle-aged adults can too. An unemployed friend demonstrated this to me when we met for lunch.

Forced to change careers in midlife, my friend was now taking classes in anatomy and physiology. As we lingered over our diet sodas, she sketched on a napkin her latest lesson in the wonders and workings of the human body. As she shared her passion, our college-aged waiter couldn't help overhearing. He too was taking classes in a similar field and soon was sharing his fascination with the same subject. My friend and our waiter may not have realized it, but they were both "pondering the works of the Lord."

Similarly, new Christians aren't the only ones who can have a sense of wonder in God and His works; longtime Christians can, too. Just as the wonder of human physiology is never ending, the wonder of God also never ends. Why not focus today on one thing about our Almighty God that absolutely fascinates you? See if that doesn't ignite a new spark in your relationship with the mighty Creator of the universe.

O God, Creator of Heaven and earth, You are so awesome! I'll need an eternity in Heaven to have enough time to praise and honor and adore You—and to explore the marvelous wonders of Your works. I can't wait! In the holy name of Jesus, my Lord and Savior, I pray. Amen.

Never-Ending Light of the World

And God said, "Let there be light," and there was light (Genesis 1:3).

Scripture: Genesis 1:1-5
Song: "Light of the World"

In the book of Genesis, we learn that God created light on the first day. This light was not the sun, moon, or stars; those celestial lights were created on the fourth day. What was this source of light? Revelation 22:5, where the new Jerusalem is described, says: "There will be no more night. They will not need the light of a lamp or the light of the sun, for the Lord God will give them light." The *Contemporary English Version* puts it like this: "The Lord God will be their light." In other words, the light is God himself.

This world is a dark place, but Christians need never fear stumbling around in its darkness—not when we have the light of God. Just as the blanket of night recedes with the rising of the sun, once His light shines on something, the darkness departs. Furthermore, the light of God is eternal, with us from the beginning of our Christian walk to the end of this earthly life and beyond.

Someday there will be no need for the sun, only the Son who says in John 8:12: "I am the light of the world. Whoever follows me will never walk in darkness, but will have the light of life."

Almighty and most merciful God, truly You are the light of my life. I'm thankful for the light You shed on all the dark corners of my life. Thank You that, unlike the sun, which one day will cease to exist, Your light is never-ending. In the name of the Father, the Son, and the Holy Spirit, I pray. Amen.

The King of the Earth

He sits enthroned above the circle of the earth, and its people are like grasshoppers. He stretches out the heavens like a canopy, and spreads them out like a tent to live in (Isaiah 40:22).

Scripture: Isaiah 40:21-26
Song: "All Creatures of Our God and King"

"Grasshopper" is a good description of what I felt like on a visit to Germany. At one point our trip took us through the Swiss Alps, via the Autobahn. Rather than going over the mountains, this highway snakes around the bottom of narrow valley floors. It is a very humbling experience to stand at the bottom of a range of snow-capped mountains towering 10,000 feet above you. I felt very small.

Ever since that trip, I can easily visualize God, sitting on top of those mountains, on His majestic throne, looking down on His "grasshoppers." But do you somehow feel less valuable being grouped with insects? Don't be. An important point comes later in our Scripture reading: "He who brings out the starry host one by one, and calls them each by name. Because of His great power and mighty strength, not one of them is missing" (Isaiah 40:26). We may be "grasshoppers," but God knows each one of us by name. And because of His power and strength, not one of us is "missing" from His care.

Father God, thank You for caring for your creation—including stars, grasshoppers, and people. You alone deserve to sit enthroned over all. How comforting and humbling to know that amidst all the billions of people that have lived—past, present, and future—You love me enough to know my name. Thank You, in Jesus' name. Amen.

The Parenting Desert

John wore clothing made of camel's hair, with a leather belt around his waist, and he ate locusts and wild honey (Mark 1:6).

Scripture: Mark 1:1-8
Song: "Does Jesus Care?"

Have you ever wondered what it would have been like to parent a prophet like John the Baptist? From a mother's point of view, I'm guessing Elizabeth struggled with her son living in a desert, eating locusts and wild honey, and wearing woven camel hair clothing. She probably never once looked at the man without seeing the boy she'd swaddled, nursed, comforted, trained, and taught. As a father it must have been bittersweet for Zechariah to see his son faithfully living out his dedicated, sacrificial life, knowing that perhaps great suffering lay ahead. But was their biggest struggle the realization that their child belonged to God first and that he was just "on loan" to them from Heaven for a brief time?

When we first bring a child into this world, we don't know how that life will unfold. Because of recorded history, we know of John's tragic, but ultimately triumphant end. But Elizabeth and Zechariah couldn't know that, not at first. They just did what all godly parents do: raised their child to the best of their ability and then put him back into the Lord's hands. (Perhaps we are not so different from John's parents after all.)

O God, I pray for all those parents who have had to give up a child, whether through death, waywardness, or just growing up and moving away. I thank You that when we give back our children to You, You are worthy of that trust. In Jesus' name, amen.

Mankind's Greatest Treasure

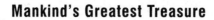

**He said to them, "This is what I told you while I was still with you: Everything must be fulfilled that is written about me in the Law of Moses, the Prophets and the Psalms."
Then He opened their minds so they could understand the Scriptures** (Luke 24:44, 45).

Scripture: Luke 24:44-49
Song: "Thy Word"

Not long ago, my aunt showed me a treasure that once belonged to my grandfather—a family Bible. Eager to make a sentimental connection with my long-dead relative, I carefully opened the 150-year-old leather-bound volume. A thrill went through me as I scanned the first page . . . then a sense of disappointment arose. The Bible was a treasure in that it once belonged to my grandfather, but it was unusable to me because I couldn't understand a word of it. It was written in Swedish.

Imagine the joy of the disciples when Jesus opened their minds to understand what the Jewish people had been reading and debating for centuries in the Scriptures. At last, prophetic passages made sense. It must have seemed as if Jesus handed them a key to unlock mankind's greatest treasure, God's Word.

Before becoming a Christian I remember trying to read the Bible. It was just like trying to decipher my grandfather's Swedish—it made no sense to me at all. Now, through the power of the Holy Spirit, when I read Scripture, it is as life-sustaining to me as the air I breathe.

Lord, thank You for Your Word. I couldn't live one day without it. Thank You for giving me the key to understanding Your Word— the Holy Spirit. In Jesus' name, amen.

Just Like John

There came a man who was sent from God; his name was John. He came as a witness to testify concerning that light, so that through him all men might believe. He himself was not the light; he came only as a witness to the light (John 1:6-8).

Scripture: John 1:1-14
Song: "Voice of Truth"

When I think of John the Baptist, the image of a unique spiritual giant comes to mind. But John and the modern-day Christian do share some common ground. John's job while on earth was to point the way to Christ, and he fulfilled that. True, he was single-minded in his purpose. He lived in the desert with no roof over his head. He fed and clothed himself using resources from nature; therefore, he had no use for money or a job. Also, he had no wife or children depending on him.

Few of us in modern times feel we could "connect" with someone like John; we have jobs and mortgages and spouses and children to divide our focus. But, as our verse says, John was a witness, and he was sent by God. Isn't that the calling of all of us Christians? Aren't we sent by God to the people in our lives—to be witnesses and testify to the salvation available through Christ? We'll never get our lives written up in Scripture, but we have everything that John had; namely, an assignment from God and the power of the Holy Spirit to carry it out.

Father God, sometimes when I read about the spiritual giants of the Bible, I feel inferior. Help me to realize that the people in the Bible were much like me. Your presence in their lives is what made them extraordinary. In Jesus' name I pray. Amen.

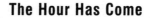

The Hour Has Come

Father, the hour has come; glorify thy Son that the Son may glorify thee (John 17:1, *Revised Standard Version*).

Scripture: John 17:1-5
Song: "Battle Hymn of the Republic"

I have the good fortune to be a member of the so-called "Greatest Generation" (Tom Brokaw's words, not mine). Of course, we were far from perfect, but as I read this passage from the Gospel of John, I thought of my young friends and classmates, ages about 19–23, many decades ago. Jesus prayed to His Father to glorify Him as He willingly went to the cross. My contemporaries also willingly went to their own glory. Among them were 22 members of my college class who without reservation embarked on treacherous paths from which they did not return. One of those 22 men received the Congressional Medal of Honor, the highest medal for heroism in battle.

As we meditate on this part of Jesus' final prayer, we note that He defines eternal life not as an endless *quantity* of time, but as a *quality* of relationship—being ever in relationship with the persons of the Trinity. Jesus glorified His Father by accomplishing the work the Father gave Him to do. I believe that our benevolent Father looks upon my fallen classmates—as well as all the others who have given their lives in sacrifice for others —as having, in some significant way, also glorified Him.

Father, look upon the men and women who serve in the armed forces of their country with Your heavenly grace as they seek Your glory. Through Christ, amen.

March 12–18. **Phillips Huston** is a retired magazine editor and writer living with his wife, Ruthann, in Naples, Florida.

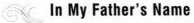

In My Father's Name

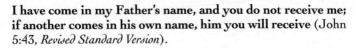

I have come in my Father's name, and you do not receive me; if another comes in his own name, him you will receive (John 5:43, *Revised Standard Version*).

Scripture: John 5:39-47
Song: "Father, Make Us One"

Man is a cynical beast, always has been. "Of course, the earth is flat; see the edge out there?" "A self-propelled boat? That's Mr. Fulton's Folly." "Flying is for birds, not those two brothers; they're bicycle mechanics." But when Columbus, Robert Fulton, and the Wright Brothers proved their cases, the opposition melted away.

Not so in Jesus' day. When Jesus made His case that He was the Son of the Father, His opponents refused to accept it. Jesus cited the testimony of John the Baptist and the many works and signs the Father had sent Him to do. He even cited the words of their beloved Moses. Many people of that day accepted false Messiahs who came in their own names, but they just couldn't accept that Jesus was the source of eternal life. So the chosen people, by and large, chose to revel in disbelief.

Nor are false prophets unknown in our time. They come in many forms on the television screen, in the sports arena, in the social setting. But unlike the scribes and Pharisees who refused to accept Jesus as the Messiah, let us pray to keep our minds and hearts open to Him.

Heavenly Father, help us to keep the pleasures of secular entertainment in perspective, never forgetting that You and Your Son are the truth. You call for much more of our attention than anything else. In the name of Jesus, the Messiah, I pray. Amen.

Who Says So?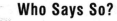

Jesus answered them, "My teaching is not mine, but his who sent me" (John 7:16, *Revised Standard Version*).

Scripture: John 7:10-18
Song: "Book of Books, Our People's Strength"

Adelia Brier, Minnie Lloyd, Roy Welch. Do the names mean anything to you? No, nor would my name mean anything to them. These were three teachers—one each from grammar school, high school, and college—among many whose dedication and enthusiasm made a lasting impact on me. Those folks have enriched my life over the decades. What a worthwhile calling!

Jesus thought so too. Throughout the Gospels He taught regularly. When He went to the Feast of the Tabernacles, He sneaked into Jerusalem so as not to make a big splash, then confronted His adversaries head-on. He began teaching in the temple, and some of the Jews marveled and asked, "How is it that this man has learning when He has never studied?" They meant that He had never formally studied the rabbinical canons these teachers relied on. But He didn't need to. Jesus made it clear His authority came from God.

We all are teachers in some sense. Some in the schoolroom, some in Sunday School, some on the ball field, some in the kitchen. However advanced or humble, we can follow the example of the rabbi from Nazareth. We can ask His Father for guidance in one of life's most challenging and meaningful tasks.

Heavenly Father, invest with Your authority and wisdom those persons entrusted with the formation of young minds (and older ones too). In Jesus' name, amen.

Before Abraham Was

Jesus said to them, "Truly, truly, I say to you, before Abraham was, I am" (John 8:58, *Revised Standard Version*).

Scripture: John 8:48-59
Song: "The God of Abraham Praise"

I didn't understand all the theories and formulas described in Walter Isaacson's monumental biography of Albert Einstein, but I developed a profound interest in the man through the book. He was reared an Orthodox Jew and exhibited no belief in the divinity of Jesus, but he was no atheist. He sometimes called God "the Old One." The man, who knew more about space, time, matter, and energy than anyone else, acknowledged that God was, and is, the architect of it all. As Einstein put it, "The Old One doesn't play dice with the universe." In other words, God has a plan, and we are part of it. But what Einstein didn't acknowledge was this: Jesus is the centerpiece of the plan.

In this era of excitement over space exploration and deep probes by the Hubble telescope, we must keep in the forefront of our minds Jesus' amazing declaration: He was with the Father before the world existed.

The religious leaders of the day sneered, "Are you greater than our Father Abraham who died?" He replied that their father Abraham rejoiced to see Jesus' day. After all, said Jesus, "Before Abraham was, I am."

That was too much. They picked up stones to throw at Him.

O God, the King of glory, help me keep my focus on the timeless Jesus and the eternal truth amid the excitement of the Space Age. In the name of the Father, the Son, and the Holy Spirit, I pray. Amen.

A Matter of Priorities

They loved the praise of men more than the praise of God (John 12:43, *Revised Standard Version*).

Scripture: John 12:36-43
Song: "Spread, O Spread, Thou Mighty Word"

At our church in New England, the 8:00 AM service was sometimes called "The Golfers' Service." Some of those who attended it were very good golfers, but they were even better Christians. They love the game and enjoy it on Sundays, but they love God first. (I will leave it up to you to decide whether they ought to play on weekdays instead.)

I wish I would see more of my friends, especially men, in our pews on Sundays. And not just golfers, but those who wouldn't miss "Meet the Press" or can't wait to get started on the Sunday newspaper's crossword puzzle. These are "good guys" by the usual criteria, but in the words of this reading from John's Gospel, perhaps they love the praise of men more than the praise of God.

This isn't just a contemporary attitude. The Gospel tells us that even some of the authoritative men of Jesus' time believed in Him but were afraid to confess it. They feared the Pharisees, even though the model for them (and for us) was Jesus, whose glory came through selfless surrender. He could have chosen to avoid the cross, but for our sakes He didn't.

Of course, this comes back to me. Have I really tried to show my absent friends the glory that comes from God?

Heavenly Father, help me shed the inhibitions that keep me from being an effective missionary among my peers. Through Christ, amen.

That We All Be One

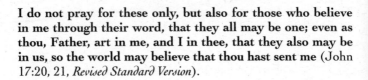

I do not pray for these only, but also for those who believe in me through their word, that they all may be one; even as thou, Father, art in me, and I in thee, that they also may be in us, so the world may believe that thou hast sent me (John 17:20, 21, *Revised Standard Version*).

Scripture: John 17:20-24
Song: "The Church's One Foundation"

To put this passage in context, let's examine what comes immediately before and after it. Following verses 20-24 comes John's account of the trial and crucifixion. Jesus knows the cross is looming. Prior to the passage, He prayed first to His Father, then for His disciples. In this passage He prays for the people who have been brought into the fold by His disciples. That's us, folks. He prays for the unity of all who believe in Him, using the unity of Father and Son as the model.

Paul got it right when he stressed bringing the message of Jesus to Jews and Gentiles alike. But after him we Christians haven't done all that well in pursuing Christ's ideal of unity over the succeeding 20 centuries, have we? Schisms, factions, sects, theological nitpicks, divisions between and within denominations have seriously splintered us. Some of those who leave or change or start anew find spiritual rewards. Many don't and drift farther away. Thus it must be a crushing disappointment to Jesus that so many have not followed His call to unity.

Dear Father, when petty squabbles erupt in our church lives, help me to be a steadying force and be reminded of Your Son's prayer for the unity of His followers. In the name of Jesus, Lord and Savior of all, I pray. Amen.

It's a Miracle!

This, the first of his signs, Jesus did at Cana in Galilee, and manifested his glory; and his disciples believed in him (John 2:11, *Revised Standard Version*).

Scripture: John 2:1-12
Song: "It Took a Miracle"

We often use the word *miracle* loosely to describe a happy outcome, prayed for or not. Recently, a daughter and grand-daughter were visiting our home, and we set out for a morning at the zoo. Almost immediately there was a clunk, clunk, clunk. A flat? No, the tires were inflated. "Miracle" #1: A good guy heard the clunking, was curious, drove up, crawled under the car, discovered a loose part dragging on the road, got tools, reat-tached it. "Miracle" #2: It happened inside our community; an-other 50 yards and we'd have been on a six-lane highway during morning rush hour. These were miracles with a small "m."

Turning water into wine at the feast at Cana was the first among many true miracles performed by Jesus. It took place at a party among presumably healthy people. No one was dead, paralyzed, starving, or handicapped—only embarrassed. So, was Jesus just "practicing" before He performed such momen-tous feats as raising Lazarus from the dead or feeding the 5,000? Of course not! Among the wedding guests were His disciples; this was an opportunity to manifest His glory. His disciples be-lieved; the miracle helped establish His following among them.

Heavenly Father, although we are awed by the many miracles You performed through Your Son, we can't always expect miraculous answers to our prayers. Help us to accept no or wait as part of Your plan for us too. In Jesus' name, amen.

Light of Hope

You are the light of the world. A city on a hill cannot be hidden (Matthew 5:14).

Scripture: Matthew 5:13-16
Song: "The Solid Rock"

Once while serving in the armed forces, my husband and I traveled by car through unknown territory to a military base. The map in hand served as our main source of information, along with a radio, which warned of an impending snowstorm.

As the night closed in around us, we drove into the storm. We felt alone. We saw no other cars on the road, and there was no sign of houses on this long stretch of highway. We anxiously strained our eyes, trying to see through the now blinding snow, praying to see lights from a house, a store, or a town.

When lights did appear in our blurred vision, we couldn't tell if they were from a vehicle or from something else just ahead. We were relieved when we realized the lights came from a town, and we had reached a safe place.

Jesus tells us to be lights for others to see so that they may come to Him and receive hope. My husband and I were thankful for the lights of the town on that snowy night; they brought us to a safe place. We are thankful for the "lights" of others who continue to shine forth to us what a life in Christ looks like.

My Father in Heaven, I want to be a light that is not hidden. In the words I speak and in all the decisions I make, let me be a shining witness to others of Your goodness and love. In the name of Your Son, my Savior, I pray. Amen.

March 19–25. **Beverly LaHote Schwind** is an author, nurse, and grandmother of 14, living in Fairfield Glade, Tennessee. She and her husband have won many medals in Senior Olympics.

Light Conquers

For all of them, deep darkness is their morning; they make friends with the terrors of darkness (Job 24:17).

Scripture: Job 24:13-17
Song: "In Christ Alone"

I heard a strange noise in the middle of the night. I couldn't identify it, but I knew there was something going on somewhere in the house. We turned on all the lights and walked cautiously, room by room. When we found nothing unusual, we turned off the lights and went back to bed. Yet I continued to lie awake, listening for sounds of an intruder.

The strange noise continued until one night the scary imagined "intruder"—a tiny mouse—was caught. Finally, we were able to take control of the night invader who hid during the day, perhaps watching me as I went about the house.

Not only noises arise during the night. Sometimes dark thoughts bubble up too. Bad experiences can run through our minds as if we were sitting in a movie theater watching the experience play out before us. And reoccurring nightmares can jerk us awake in the dark of the night. But the light of day brings relief.

In the same way, the thief comes at night so he will not be easily seen and recognized. He can hide in the shadows. But Jesus is our light. He keeps us from fears of the night. He brings clarity to a dark situation as we focus on Him. Bottom line: Light conquers darkness.

Thank You, **Jesus,** for being the light in my life, for leading me through the fears that come to me, especially in the dark of night. In Your precious name I pray. Amen.

 Praise in the Shelter

I will praise you forever for what you have done; in your name I will hope, for your name is good. I will praise you in the presence of your saints (Psalm 52:9).

Scripture: Psalm 52
Song: "Amazing Grace"

My husband and I enjoy doing work at our local homeless shelter. Once a month, we take a meal in and lead a devotional service. One night more children were present than usual. When I asked what song they would like to sing, I thought it would be "Jesus Loves Me." But to my surprise, they asked for "Amazing Grace." I called the younger children to the front of the small church, and they led the singing.

The people at the shelter are truly thankful for the food and housing that they receive. And they're quick to get up and testify about what God has done for them.

When we ask for prayer requests or praise reports, the men eagerly step to their feet, telling how God provides, and then they pray for one another. Perhaps they arrived at the homeless shelter after losing a job or suffering some other calamity, or after making a series of poor choices. But now they recognize the blessings they receive as a result of prayer.

Sometimes things have happened in my life that I did not consider a blessing at all. But later I was moved to praise Him for what happened. The door opened, so I could reap the benefit God intended for me.

I praise You, **Lord,** for all Your goodness to me. I know You have a plan for me, though sometimes I don't understand. Keep me faithful, through Christ I pray. Amen.

Look to the Redeemer

Moses made a bronze snake and put it up on a pole. Then when anyone was bitten by a snake and looked at the bronze snake, he lived (Numbers 21:9).

Scripture: Numbers 21:4-9
Song: "Jesus Only Let Me See"

When I graduated from nursing school, I received a special pin to put on my cap or uniform. The pin showed a pole with a serpent wrapped around it. This image has been a symbol of healing from the time of Moses. Because Moses' people disobeyed God, snakes began to bite and kill them. The people repented, and God told Moses to have them look to the bronze pole so they could be healed.

The very serpents that plagued the people now became their symbol of hope, a very real refuge. So the people did as they were told. And as they looked to the pole as God had commanded them, they lived. They looked at the image of evil that hurt them—but now, through the power of God, evil would bow to a merciful, redemptive purpose.

Sometimes I have to look at what is hurting me and ask God how I can cope with it. I must look the problem in the face and deal with it directly, moving through the pain rather than simply avoiding it. None of us can bring about healing and salvation by ourselves. But through our "lifted up" Christ, our great Redeemer, all things are possible.

Lord, thank You that You became my Healer. When I look to You, as I am told to do, I receive healing in my spirit, which I need. I praise You, because You have made provision for me to look to You for all my needs. Through Christ I pray. Amen.

Treasured Heirloom

He broke into pieces the bronze snake Moses had made, for up to that time the Israelites had been burning incense to it (2 Kings 18:4).

Scripture: 2 Kings 18:1-7
Song: "Heal Us, Emmanuel"

Among the things my husband found while cleaning out his desk was a rabbit's foot. People often carry a rabbit's foot for good luck. I don't understand that, since the particular rabbit clearly didn't experience good luck (no doubt the hunter did).

I also receive e-mails that tell me I must pass a message, prayer, or picture on to 10 people—so I will receive good luck, or "a blessing." If I do not pass it on, the sender warns "something bad will happen."

When King Hezekiah destroyed all the idols his people worshipped, he also destroyed the bronze pole and snake that Moses made at God's command. Hezekiah's predecessors had turned this healing image into an idol. Worshipping this treasured heirloom became more important to them than worshipping the Almighty One whose power it represented!

But we can have idols in our lives too. In fact, anything I put in God's place is an idol.

My friend felt she was to launch into a specific outreach ministry, but then a great job came along, and she put off the call to dedicated service. Years later she acknowledged that the other job had become her idol; she had forgotten God for a time.

O God, I don't want anything I have to mean more to me than You do. But it's always a temptation to move You from the center of my life. Help me, through Christ. Amen.

Instruction Book

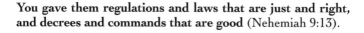

You gave them regulations and laws that are just and right, and decrees and commands that are good (Nehemiah 9:13).

Scripture: Nehemiah 9:9-15
Song: "O God, Our Help in Ages Past"

I received a booklet of instructions to follow when I began teaching in a rehab center. Although I didn't understand all of the rules, I knew they were to be followed by both teacher and residents. Certainly we appreciated the information, for now I knew what was expected of me—and of the students. Weeks later, residents of the rehab center also shared how they were helped by observing these regulations.

My father always followed certain rules when planting his garden. As a child I couldn't comprehend why he carefully lined up each row with a string and kept a "just right" space between each plant. But I understood the reason for his rules when the day came to cultivate the crops. That's when he pushed the tiller down one row and then another, without disturbing the tender plants on either side.

The prophet Ezra proclaimed the great miracles of God to his people, how God showed mercy when they repented of their sins. Yes, the Israelites knew the rules and instructions, but failed to obey them. Ezra reminded them how God led Moses and the people out of bondage in Egypt and into the promised land. Finally, as Ezra read the Scriptures aloud, the people understood and repented.

Father, thank You for Your Word, the instruction book for my life. Help me as I continue on this journey to follow the directions set down for me. In Jesus' name, amen.

Nighttime Story

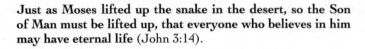

Just as Moses lifted up the snake in the desert, so the Son of Man must be lifted up, that everyone who believes in him may have eternal life (John 3:14).

Scripture: John 3:11-21
Song: "Blessed Assurance"

Our children always wanted to hear a story when we put them to bed at night. Sometimes it was a book to be read or a "tell us about when you were little" request.

They enjoyed hearing about things we'd done as children — especially if we had been in trouble! Just before leaving the room, we'd turn on a night-light.

Nicodemus came to Jesus at night to ask Him some questions. Jesus told him the story of Moses in the desert lifting up the bronze snake on a pole, and how the people who looked to it were healed. Jesus told Nicodemus that He, Jesus, would be lifted up too. All who looked to Him would be saved. In this moment Jesus illuminated the Scriptures and revealed the truth of God's profound love for the whole world.

At the church where we slept while on a mission trip in Arizona, we learned that all the kitchen articles were kept in the refrigerator: silverware, plates, and all foods. In the daylight the kitchen looked fine, but at night when we entered the room and turned on the lights, roaches scattered like spilled grain. Once again, the light revealed the evil of the darkness.

Jesus, I thank You for what You did for me on the cross. You have given me eternal life by trusting in You. You have taken the darkness out of my days and offered me a light of hope. You are the light in the night, my night-light. In Your name, amen.

Our Guiding Light

Send forth your light and your truth, let them guide me; let them bring me to your holy mountain, to the place where you dwell (Psalm 43:3).

Scripture: Psalm 43
Song: "Show Me Your Glory"

Everyone goes through struggles in their lives. For newly baptized Christians, the worries and concerns of this life seem to come almost as soon as the water has dried. It is then that believers begin to see where their faith truly lies. Or was the decision for Christ merely a "Get out of Hell Free" card?

Even King David, whom God called a man after His own heart, faced great difficulties and questioned God about getting through this life. Someone wanted him dead, and David wasn't sure he'd make it.

But David cried out to God for direction. How many of us, when we feel lost, wondering what to do next, turn to God first for guidance? Or do we look to some other "GPS" for direction? Scripture tells us that trials will come, but we are called to rejoice in the midst of them, because we know "that the testing of [our] faith develops perseverance" (James 1:3).

While we may not recognize it at the time, God is doing His work in us, refining us for His purposes, as we go through the toughest of times. That is worth rejoicing about!

Lord, may I quickly turn to You for guidance in my time of need. You know what is best for me, and I praise You for refining me to do Your will. Through Christ, amen.

March 26–31. **John Oxford** has worked as a newspaper reporter in Moultrie, Georgia, for six years. An Atlanta native, he is happily married to his wife, Ashleigh.

One of a Kind

Among the gods there is none like you, O LORD; no deeds can compare with yours (Psalm 86:8).

Scripture: Psalm 86:8-13
Song: "No One Like You"

Our world is always trying to make Jesus just another in a line of deities that people may choose to worship. People seem to be OK with saying the name of God with reverence. But how often do people cringe just in hearing the name "Jesus Christ" spoken with the reverence His name deserves? Furthermore, how willing are we to speak the name of Jesus to others, even in casual conversations?

But let us be proud of Jesus. He's still alive, after all, making Him rather unique! If you look up the prophet Mohammed of the Muslim religion, you will eventually find something on the Al-Masjid al-Nabawi Mosque in Saudi Arabia, his burial place. An Internet search of Gautama Buddha reveals there is a temple built to house one of his teeth that was kept following his cremation. Buddhists recently held celebrations when one of Gautama's fingers was moved to another temple, along with some of his other bones.

How do those, among other deities, compare to our living Lord? The other "gods" have found their final resting places. But we, the people of Jesus, are the ones who are at rest — a living, daily, restful trust in a risen Savior.

Lord, I know You are the true and living God of the universe, and I am thankful to know You as my Savior. No other gods or idols can compare to You, and for that I am eternally grateful. In the name of Jesus, Lord and Savior of all, I pray. Amen.

Meet Me at Your Table

Now Judas, who betrayed him, knew the place, because Jesus had often met there with his disciples (John 18:2).

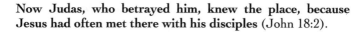

Scripture: John 18:1-11
Song: "The Motions"

Many folks intentionally avoid going to church on Sundays and shun anything that appears to be church-related. Perhaps they know they need "a good dose of Jesus," but assume it would be pretty painful.

On the other hand, I've known many seekers who've come to church as an act of desperation, as a last resort, hoping their crisis situation can be turned around. But how willing are we, as Christians, to step out of our own comfort zones and go to where those who don't yet know Jesus lives?

Judas knew where to find Jesus, but did not love Him. Do we know where to find those whom Jesus loves but do not know as disciples?

You see, because Judas had been with Jesus as an *apparent* disciple, he was able to betray Jesus. How many Christians are willing to take the other side of that and proclaim Jesus where He needs to be proclaimed?

Jesus called us to "go and make disciples of all nations, baptizing them in the name of the Father and of the Son and of the Holy Spirit" (Matthew 28:19). I know I need more boldness here. I know, too, I'm missing the great joy that comes from proclaiming His name to those who need it most.

Father, give me courage to proclaim Your name today. And help me to develop new friendships with those who still don't know You through Your Son. Amen.

Counting the Cost

"You are not one of his disciples, are you?" the girl at the door asked Peter.
He replied, "I am not" (John 18:17).

Scripture: John 18:12-18
Song: "If We Are the Body"

We don't face the possibility of death, as Peter would have, by speaking Jesus' name. Yet we too are to be His light to this world, boldly acknowledging our discipleship. As Peter came to see, the Christian faith is to be lived out, every second of every day, even amidst the most fearful circumstances.

Jesus told His disciples that the faith is much more than church attendance when He said, "Not everyone who says to me, 'Lord, Lord,' will enter the kingdom of heaven, but only he who does the will of my Father who is in heaven" (Matthew 7:21). Jesus called us to be His salt and His light in the world.

Thankfully, our Lord is also in the restoration business. Just as He forgave Peter, He will also restore us, when we fail Him, to a right relationship. I like the way writer Tim Stafford once put it: "You can worry that your relationship with [God] has gone cold, that you've lost your spiritual edge. You can think it will take a lot of time, a month or so of spiritual discipline, to get going again with Him. Then you sit down and discover, in just minutes, that you don't have to do a thing—except take some time. Be alone with Him. In what feels like no time you are caught up again in your love."

Father, I ask You to give me a heart that will be totally sold out to You and Your call in my life. I want to follow You beyond my own selfish desires. In the name of Jesus. Amen.

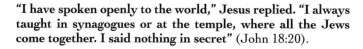

Secret Believer?

"I have spoken openly to the world," Jesus replied. **"I always taught in synagogues or at the temple, where all the Jews come together. I said nothing in secret"** (John 18:20).

Scripture: John 18:19-24
Song: "Fearless"

Jesus knew that He had spoken exactly what His Father had wanted Him to proclaim to the world. When He told the Pharisees this while He stood on "trial," He knew He was about to die the cruelest death imaginable.

For us it's different. Proclaiming His name may cost us some friends or a bit of embarrassment. Yet why are we so afraid to speak the name of Jesus openly? Sometimes I find it more comfortable to share His message with those who have never heard it than to tell my friends about Him. In fact, I'm often too content to be a secret believer.

Let us count the cost of what it means to be a disciple of Jesus. Turning our lives over to Him means facing opposition as He did. It isn't easy, but consider the rewards in the words of apostle Paul: "I have fought the good fight, I have finished the race, I have kept the faith. Now there is in store for me the crown of righteousness, which the Lord, the righteous judge, will award to me on that day—and not only me, but also to all who longed for his appearing" (2 Timothy 4:7, 8).

My Father in Heaven, I pray You will reveal yourself to me and help me remove anything from my life that hinders my relationship with You. Give me the boldness to turn from the rewards of this world and help me to see Your eternal glory. In the name of my Savior, Jesus Christ, amen.

Being and Building Disciples

To the Jews who had believed him, Jesus said, "If you hold to my teaching, you are really my disciples" (John 8:31).

Scripture: John 8:31-38
Song: "God Is Not a Secret"

Over the last couple of years, there's been a wonderful movement here in southwest Georgia. It's thrust is personal discipleship, turning men and women into true disciples of Jesus Christ. The mission has been to fully immerse believers into the Word of God, teaching them what Scriptures say, and guiding them to share the message with others. Using a Proclaim, Admonish, and Teach (PAT) method, the goal is multiplication: those who've been discipled are to find another whom they, in turn, can teach and train in the ways of practical daily kingdom living.

What does it mean to be a disciple? In reality, it's more than just coming to the faith. Jesus taught His disciples for three years before the Holy Spirit came upon them at Pentecost. But then they proclaimed His message boldly for the rest of their lives.

They were set apart from the world because, as Jesus said in our verse today, His disciples held to His teaching. Here in southwest Georgia, I've seen some 300 men and women who have heard His teaching and are spreading it around to their cities and towns and into new cities and towns. It's inspiring to see—men and women fully immersed in Christ's teachings and ready to share Him with the world.

Lord, I pray You make me into one of Your dedicated disciples. I am ready to be immersed in You, and I want to teach others about You too. In Jesus' name, amen.

DEVOTIONS®

APRIL

Whoever drinks the water I give him will never thirst. Indeed, the water I give him will become in him a spring of water welling up to eternal life.

—John 4:14

Gary Allen, Editor   **Margaret Williams,** Project Editor   Photo by Jupiterimages/Comstock/Thinkstock®

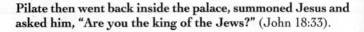

You Are My King

Pilate then went back inside the palace, summoned Jesus and asked him, "Are you the king of the Jews?" (John 18:33).

Scripture: John 18:28-38
Song: "We Wear His Name"

That is the question the entire world wants to know: Is Jesus really who He said He is? People either come humbly before Him or reject the Christian faith, often based on whether they can grasp the real Jesus or not.

Furthermore, would you as a believer be willing to speak His name with the authority it deserves? There are plenty of people who will speak His name in vain, but not many are willing to proclaim His name with proper reverence.

Even the demons know that the name of the Lord needs to be revered, not spoken in vain, "that at the name of Jesus every knee should bow, in heaven and on earth and under the earth," (Philippians 2:10). In the book of James, we also read that the demons shudder in their belief of God (2:19). Yet I sometimes have trouble speaking His name to my friends—who may be at their most desperate hour.

Who is He, really? It will take an eternity to begin to plumb the depths of His beautiful nature and character. One thing is certain though, even now: He is so much more than a warm, fuzzy feeling we may get for an hour on Sunday mornings.

Lord, I pray that You reveal Yourself to me more and more, and that I will be Your light to this dark world. In Jesus' name I pray. Amen.

April 1. **John Oxford** has worked as a newspaper reporter in Moultrie, Georgia, for six years. An Atlanta native, he is happily married to his wife, Ashleigh.

Amazing Grace

This is a faithful saying, and worthy of all acceptation, that Christ Jesus came into the world to save sinners; of whom I am chief (1 Timothy 1:15, *King James Version*).

Scripture: 1 Timothy 1:12-17
Song: "Wonderful Grace of Jesus"

John lost his mother at a young age, dropped out of school after a couple of years, and went to sea when he was only 11- years-old. But he couldn't stand Navy discipline; he deserted, was captured, flogged, and demoted. He continued his insubordination and was transferred to a merchant slave trader.

For years he was a self-described "infidel and libertine," infamous for his profanity and debauchery. Yet all that changed during a storm at sea when he called out to the God he had so long ignored.

John Newton spent the remainder of his life as a prolific hymn writer, minister, and abolitionist. But like Paul, he always saw himself as the chief of sinners. Sometime after his 50th birthday, he penned the words that have become immortal: "Amazing grace, how sweet the sound, that saved a wretch like me."

Our lives may have followed a tragic arc like Newton's and Paul's, or we may have never received so much as a speeding ticket. But whatever our pasts—Christ Jesus came into the world to save us.

Dear Heavenly Father, let me never forget the marvelous grace of Your saving forgiveness. Praise to You, in Christ's holy name. Amen.

April 2–8. **Darlene Franklin** lives in Oklahoma City near her son's family. She is the author of 10 books and more than 150 devotionals.

Getting What You Asked For

Finally Pilate handed him over to them to be crucified (John 19:16).

Scripture: John 19:4-16
Song: "Lord, Teach Us How to Pray Aright"

After more than a decade of wearing eyeglasses from Geek Central, I rebelled. I wanted to wear contact lenses at my wedding, so when a local optometrist advertised a sale, I made an appointment.

After the warning that contacts take getting used to, I wasn't surprised when my eyes smarted after the first two hours. I took them out, anointed my eyes with drops, and waited until morning. Second day, the same result. A month later, I gritted my teeth and wore them for six hours at a time—although they hurt like crazy.

My mother laughed at my vanity and told me the contacts "looked strange." After two months, even I had to admit the experiment had failed. My poor astigmatic eyes couldn't handle the contacts I had purchased . . . so I went back to glasses.

Like me and those lenses, Pilate knew the Jews were asking for the wrong thing. Jesus had done nothing deserving of death. But the crowd repeatedly asked for crucifixion, and Pilate gave in. He gave them what they asked for.

We think we know what will be good for us and for others. Without the corrective lenses of God's saving grace, we all join the ranks of those demanding the death of the Son of God.

Lord, teach me to look for Your provision and not to demand You supply my personal shopping list. I pray this prayer in the name of Jesus, my Savior and Lord. Amen.

Grading on a Curve

Anyone who blasphemes the name of the LORD must be put to death. The entire assembly must stone him. Whether an alien or native-born, when he blasphemes the Name, he must be put to death (Leviticus 24:16).

Scripture: Leviticus 24:10-16
Song: "My God, How Perfect Are Thy Ways!"

I loved school, a place where I could achieve success. The common practice of grading on the curve suited me, since that almost always guaranteed me top marks in the class.

As an employee I don't care for grading on a curve. Self-evaluation forms that ask "how do you rate yourself on a scale of 1–10 in performance?" make me shudder. Who wants to rate themselves either too low or too high?

God doesn't use a curve when it comes to keeping the law. He doesn't say, "As long as you keep my law 70% of the time, I will forgive you the other 30%."

No, God is an all-or-nothing Lord. In the progress of revelation at this time in the history of God's people, the Lord was teaching of His absolute holiness. It was a hard lesson to learn, but someday Christ would come, our substitute righteousness.

Yes, Jesus came to be the way to this holy God—the only perfect way for a world of sinners. As Thomas à Kempis once said: "Without the way, there is no going; without the truth, there is no knowing; without the life, there is no living."

O Lord, Your Law of the Old Covenant showed our ancestors the truths of holiness. Thank You for the New Covenant and its gracious offer of holiness through another way, by faith in Your own Son, Jesus. In His name I offer profound thanks. Amen.

Her Little Child

Near the cross of Jesus stood his mother, his mother's sister, Mary the wife of Clopas, and Mary Magdalene (John 19:25).

Scripture: John 19:17-25
Song: "Near the Cross"

The screen at the front of the church displayed a picture of Mary at the cross while the praise team sang about her child. Mom and I clutched each other close until grief overtook us and the tears flowed. You see, on that same day, my precious daughter's body lay in a morgue. A scant six days had passed since police had found her dead in her apartment, her neck broken and bruised. *O, Mary. How you must have wept.*

I had studied the physical agonies that crucifixion involved—scourging, nails through the hands and feet, asphyxiation mixed with unimaginable pain. But I never really felt it, not until my own dear child died.

God himself, on the cross, for me. Two parents—His heavenly Father and His earthly mother—watched in soul-rending grief. Here was the "sword [that] will pierce your own soul" (Luke 2:35), the one Simeon predicted of the baby Jesus.

As we approach Resurrection Sunday, let us join Mary at the foot of the cross . . . and weep. Bare our inmost pain and grief and loss, for "by his wounds we are healed" (Isaiah 53:5).

Dear Father, I know the grief of losing a child to untimely death. Please comfort my heart this day. Yet Your Son suffered more than physical death. In His perfection He took upon Him the world's sins and willingly, humbly, united His divine nature with human nature. How He loved me! In His name, amen.

In God's Hands

Into your hands I commit my spirit; redeem me, O LORD, the God of truth (Psalm 31:5).

Scripture: Psalm 31:1-5
Song: "Children of the Heavenly Father"

The words of the psalmist only served to mock me as I went to bed late and awoke early, the pressure of my circumstances bearing down on me. When I had taken refuge in the Lord, I had still been forced out of my marriage. When I had asked not to be put to shame, I had nevertheless landed in a legal battle that lasted for years. When I asked for freedom from an abusive marriage, both my children lived with other people until the state deemed me a fit mother.

The circumstances tempted me to despair. But my heart and my spirit belonged to the Lord, and I committed myself to Him all the more, with each passing day. I trusted that, in His time and with His truth, He would redeem and restore what I had lost.

That day did come when first my daughter, then my son, came home. What a glorious reunion!

We know Jesus asked to be spared the cup of His suffering and death. But He accepted the trial as God's will and committed His spirit to His father. He wasn't required to be happy with the situation—only to walk through it with trust in the Father.

Almighty and most merciful God, help me to remember that when trials come—and I know they will—I can rest in your arms and that You will carry me until the day of redemption comes. In the meantime, let me emulate Your sterling character, even in the most difficult situations. In the name of Christ I pray. Amen.

Do It Now

Later, Joseph of Arimathea asked Pilate for the body of Jesus. Now Joseph was a disciple of Jesus, but secretly because he feared the Jews. With Pilate's permission, he came and took the body away (John 19:38).

Scripture: John 19:38-42
Song: "Time, by Moments, Steals Away"

Friday night after work I headed for the building's exit. A tiny part of me dreamed that my daughter would be waiting for me. Her joyous call of "Mom!" would greet me, and she would crush me in her embrace. How many times had I received such a greeting? How little had I valued those moments?

But Jolene wouldn't be there this Friday night, or any day in the future. In a brief, brutal act, she snuffed out her life and much of my joy.

In life, struggling with mental anguish, Jolene could be demanding and irritating. But after her death, I keenly felt the loss of her exuberant expressions of love. All the things that drove me to distraction faded away as unimportant.

Death has a way of bringing our true emotions into focus. During Jesus' life, Joseph of Arimathea followed Him secretly. At His death, Joseph went public. He asked Pilate for permission to bury the body; he carried it away and buried it in his own tomb. All the reasons for keeping quiet faded in the stark pain of losing the Messiah.

Dear Lord, like Joseph, I may sometimes wait too long to demonstrate my love for those dearest to me. Remind me of the fleeting hours and the fragility of my own days. Let me speak today, while I still have time. Through Christ my Lord, amen.

Lessons from Mother Goose

He saw the strips of linen lying there, as well as the burial cloth that had been around Jesus' head. The cloth was folded up by itself, separate from the linen (John 20:6, 7).

Scripture: John 20:1-10, 19, 20
Song: "Lead Me to Calvary"

On Easter Sunday I pulled into a parking space at church and got out of the car. A goose ran in front of me, hissing. The reason for his panic became evident: four eggs sat in a nest located only a few feet from the church's front door.

Fascinated by live Easter eggs, everyone—from the youngest child to the oldest patriarch—kept a "birth watch" for several weeks. The mama goose laid two more eggs before she began sitting on the nest.

Early in May, the eggs hatched, and I drove into the parking lot, hoping for a glimpse of the babies. The nest lay there . . . empty. Of the mother, father, and babies—no sign. In the habit of geese, they had moved their goslings to new territory.

We had awaited their arrival. We knew they had come alive because they had left evidence of their former existence behind.

When John and Peter ran to the tomb that resurrection morning, they found not a dead body—but what Jesus had left behind when He arose from the dead. John understood and believed the evidence of the clothes left behind.

All praise to You, **Savior!** I am so thankful that I can look to the empty tomb to know that You are alive. Even more wonderful, You have promised to indwell my very being through Your Spirit within me. May I live gratefully in Your love this day. In the holy name of Jesus I pray. Amen.

Love Always Obeys

So now I charge you in the sight of all Israel and of the assembly of the LORD, and in the hearing of our God: Be careful to follow all the commands of the LORD your God, that you may possess this good land and pass it on as an inheritance to your descendants forever (1 Chronicles 28:8).

Scripture: 1 Chronicles 28:1-10
Song: "Love the Lord Your God"

As I said good night to my daughter, I asked her whether she'd finished her homework. She said, "Yes."

The following day I received a phone call from her English teacher informing me that she never turned in her essay. So that evening I asked her how her day had gone. "Fine," she mumbled, and then disappeared into her room. I waited a minute and then knocked on her door. "Yeah?" she answered. I entered and asked her, "Did you turn in your essay today?" Avoiding eye contact, she answered, "Yeah."

"Your teacher called me today," I said. My daughter's jaw dropped. I'd caught her in a lie—a breech of the Commandments—with no way out.

Our world tempts us into thinking it's no big deal. It's just a little "white lie." Just as David admonished His people to obey all of God's commands, we too are called to obedience.

Dear Lord, give me the strength to follow You today, being mindful to keep Your commands and walk in Your love, choosing life for me and my children. In the precious name of Jesus I pray. Amen.

April 9–15. **Bonnie Prestel** is a freelance writer who has just finished her first novel. She lives in Colorado Springs with her two daughters and one cat.

Down at His Feet

Let us go to his dwelling place; let us worship at his footstool (Psalm 132:7).

Scripture: Psalm 132:1-14
Song: "No Higher Calling"

"Mommy, does God live in all the churches?" asked my curious 5-year-old one morning after leaving Sunday service. I smiled at her and said, "Well, honey, we worship God in church, but He is everywhere. He lives in you and me, not in a building. He is always with us, always caring for us." That answer satisfied her curiosity, and she skipped to the car.

I grew up attending some of the most gorgeous churches — bright colors reflecting through picturesque stained glass windows, intricate wooden carvings, and red velvet carpets adorning the altar. I learned at a young age that church was a holy place: It was God's house. So, whenever I needed to talk to God I would go to the nearest church. As I grew in age and wisdom, I discovered that God is, of course, much more than a building or place. He dwells within us by His Holy Spirit.

The Scripture tells us, too, that God inhabits the praises of His people. When I go into my quiet corner of the house, focus my attention on God, and begin to worship and praise Him, I truly find Him.

As you cultivate your relationship with God, take time just to worship at His feet. There is no higher place.

Heavenly Father, I often rush through my days without spending quality quiet time with You. I desire to worship and kneel at Your feet. For You alone are worthy of all worship and praise. In the name of Jesus I pray. Amen.

Turn Back to God

If you return to the LORD, then your brothers and your children will be shown compassion by their captors and will come back to this land, for the LORD your God is gracious and compassionate. He will not turn his face from you if you return to him (2 Chronicles 30:9).

Scripture: 2 Chronicles 30:1-9
Song: "Step by Step"

One sunny Saturday in June, my girlfriend and I took a hike in the mountains. Distracted by our conversation, we veered off the trail and were soon forging our own path. At first, it looked just like the trail, but the deeper into the forest we went, obstacles emerged: boulders in this dubious "path," broken tree limbs blocking our way. We couldn't go any further without getting seriously hurt. But it was too late. Fear entered our hearts. What do we do now?

I heard a small voice say, "Turn around, walk the other way." We did—and eventually found our way back to the trail.

Isn't it quite the same with God? Often we're out doing our own thing, not even realizing that we have turned from God. But soon we're simply forging our own way. The solution is simple. Turn around and head the opposite way, back into the arms of God. He is always waiting for us and will once again embrace us in His love.

Gracious Father, sometimes I let my own ambitions lead me. And sometimes my pride takes me far away from close fellowship with You. At those times, please help me to turn around and acknowledge you in all my ways. Direct my path and bring me home to safety. I pray all this through Your Son, my Savior. Amen.

Our Safe Place

May there be peace within your walls and security within your citadels (Psalm 122:7).

Scripture: Psalm 122
Song: "Strong Tower"

Old houses creak. When my daughters and I moved into our "new" house, built in 1929, we heard lots of scary noises in the night. That first night my youngest daughter came into my room whispering, "Mommy, can I sleep with you?" I pried my sleepy eyes open and saw the fear on her face. "Sure, sweetie, come on in." I folded back the covers, and she crawled in to snuggle close to me.

According to Webster's *New World Dictionary,* a citadel is a "fortress; fortified place; stronghold; a place of safety: refuge." All through the Psalms, the psalmists proclaim God as their hiding place and refuge. Most people are familiar with Psalm 91:1, 2 for instance, which proclaims: "He who dwells in the shelter of the Most High will rest in the shadow of the Almighty. I will say of the Lord, 'He is my refuge and my fortress, my God, in whom I trust.'"

I'm sure there are times—when we hear "bumps in the night"—that even we adults should simply climb into our Father's arms and make Him our safe hiding place.

Almighty and most merciful God, remind me this day that my security resides in no physical structure, government, or person. You alone are my safe place. When the darkness of night falls, I run to You, Lord, and I find peace resting in Your love. In the name of Jesus, who lives and reigns with You and the Holy Spirit, one God, now and forever, amen.

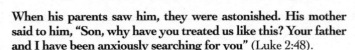

Trust God with Your Children

When his parents saw him, they were astonished. His mother said to him, "Son, why have you treated us like this? Your father and I have been anxiously searching for you" (Luke 2:48).

Scripture: Luke 2:41-51
Song: "Mary, Did You Know?"

My first summer home from college caused much conflict between my parents and me. My newfound freedom collided with their long-standing house rules. Often, I missed curfew. My dad would drive down the dark streets looking for me in the wee hours of the morning. When I returned home safely, Mom would be crying in the kitchen. "How could you do this to me? I was so worried," she cried. (And I was *not* off doing my Father's work.)

When Jesus stayed in the temple, his mother worried. She didn't yet fully understand the call on His life.

When we raise our children in the Lord, God will lead them through life, just as He has led us. We have faced risks and trials, dangers and joys—just as they will face. We may not fully understand why our children struggle, but we must remember that our children are God's children first. They belong to Him, just as we belong to Him.

When the time comes for them to go and follow God, we must let go and trust that He will take care of them. Even when we do not understand, we can trust in God's plan.

God, give me the strength to let go of my children when they choose to follow You and answer Your call in our turbulent world. In the holy name of Jesus, amen.

Our Rescuer Lives

Rescue me from the mire, do not let me sink; deliver me from those who hate me, from the deep waters (Psalm 69:14).

Scripture: Psalm 69:6-15
Song: "Great Is the Lord Almighty"

When my eldest daughter attended first grade at a small Christian school, some of the kids formed a club. To join this secret club you had to say a bad word. My daughter chose the word *ain't*, (her mom is a writer) and her best friend chose the word *hate*.

Hate is a strong word not allowed in our home. Often people throw it around as in "I hate school" or "I hate broccoli." But in Jesus' day you could be stoned if you were hated. Persecution was more than being shunned at the lunch table. In our Scripture today, David was mocked at the gate, scorned, and shamed. But he still had faith that His God would deliver Him from his enemies.

We may face persecution in the workplace or in our neighborhoods. Stating you are a Christian often comes with a price. People make fun of us. The news media sometimes caricatures us, ridiculing our so-called "extreme" worldview. And bumper stickers mock our faith, staring us in the face at every red light.

We must remember that God will never leave us or forsake us. So when it gets tough, and it will, don't forsake Him. He is our most faithful friend and deliverer.

O God, the King of glory, give me the faith and boldness and courage to stand up for You and Your ways; deliver me from those who hate me. I pray this prayer in the name of Jesus, my merciful Savior and Lord. Amen.

Passion for God

His disciples remembered that it is written: "Zeal for your house will consume me" (John 2:17).

Scripture: John 2:13-22
Song: "I Could Sing of Your Love Forever"

I met a young man who became a close brother in Christ. He chose to leave secular employment and enter Bible college. His transformation was so profound that he had Scripture tattooed all over his body and wore a T-shirt with the inscription, "Jesus Freak." He was zealous for God and clearly not ashamed to proclaim it to the world. His unique approach would speak to a certain type of person that many other believers might not reach.

The word *zeal* means "intense enthusiasm; ardent devotion, working for a cause." Jesus was zealous for His Father's house as demonstrated by His righteous anger toward the money changers. His passion for His Father consumed Him.

In today's world we witness passion and zeal for famous movie stars, football players, and people in powerful, political positions. It is rare to see zeal for Jesus. But my friend was a Jesus fanatic and not ashamed to show it.

What are you passionate about? Is it your work, your favorite sports team, or maybe a special relationship? Although these things are good, suppose we reserve our greatest passion for the things of God? Today, let's stand up and do something outrageous: serve with compassion, love without condition, witness creatively with conviction.

Gracious Father, stir up my passion for You today. Let the world see my zeal for You and Your kingdom—by the way I talk and the way I walk. In Jesus' name, amen.

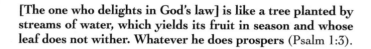

Well Watered

[The one who delights in God's law] is like a tree planted by streams of water, which yields its fruit in season and whose leaf does not wither. Whatever he does prospers (Psalm 1:3).

Scripture: Psalm 1
Song: "As a Tree Beside the Water"

The pine family of trees, made up of more than 100 species, is a wonder. Pines appear as far north as Scandinavia and as far south as Sumatra. They grow high in the Himalayas but also thrive at sea level. At 4,800 years of age, one example of the bristlecone pine near Bishop, California, is among the oldest living organisms on earth. The shortest pine may be the Siberian dwarf pine, which sometimes reaches a height of just 3 feet at maturity, while the world's tallest pine is the sugar pine, known to soar as high as 265 feet.

When it comes to the size of pines, one consistent factor is available water. A pine in a desert will be stunted, while a pine in a rainforest will grow tall and lush. It just stands to reason.

And it just stands to reason that our spiritual environment will determine our spiritual health as well. Are we living in the spiritual desert of ungodly influence? (Psalm 1:1) If so, we can expect to produce little of worth for the Lord. But if we are immersed in Scripture, like a tree's roots reaching into a flowing stream (v. 2), we will bear fruit season after season.

I want to be productive for You over the long term, **Dear Lord.** Teach me Your Word. I pray in Jesus' holy name. Amen.

April 16–22. **Eric Stanford** is an independent book editor living in Colorado Springs, Colorado. He and his wife, Elisa, have two daughters: Eden and Elizabeth.

Unquenchable Thirst

As the deer pants for streams of water, so my soul pants for you, O God (Psalm 42:1).

Scripture: Psalm 42
Song: "As the Deer"

One of the signs of the onset of Type 2 diabetes is unquenchable thirst. When diabetic thirst set in for a man named Sean, he was boarding an airplane. Before the flight even took off, he hit the call button and begged a flight attendant for a water bottle. Reluctantly, she agreed to get him one. But she had not even returned to her seat when he was pushing the button again. By the time his hour-long flight was over, a pile of empty water bottles surrounded Sean.

Are we as thirsty for God as Sean was thirsty for water on that airplane? Or are we as thirsty for God as a deer that's run a long distance in a dry landscape?

One of the common images for spiritual desire in Scripture is thirst. God bids all who are thirsty to come to Him. He calls blessed those who hunger and thirst after righteousness. He offers living water that springs up to eternal life.

That raises a question: If we don't have much thirst for Him, how do we get it? Oddly enough, by drinking.

The more we get of Him, the more we want. His water both slakes—and recreates—our thirst.

Almighty and most merciful God, I thirst for You. And I thirst to become thirstier for You. Satisfy me with Yourself—as You help me let go of so much that promises satisfaction apart from You and Your Word. In the name of the Father, the Son, and the Holy Spirit, I pray. Amen.

What the Hearer Says

The Spirit and the bride say, "Come!" And let him who hears say, "Come!" Whoever is thirsty, let him come; and whoever wishes, let him take the free gift of the water of life (Revelation 22:17).

Scripture: Revelation 22:10-17
Song: "Come, Every Soul by Sin Oppressed"

Two thousand years ago, Jesus commissioned His followers to make disciples. So let's take stock. How are we doing?

Research shows that about 55 percent of Christians in America share their faith with a non-Christian in a 12-month period. Could be worse. Could be better, too. How about you? When was the last time you shared your faith?

As we see in Revelation 22, the Holy Spirit calls all people to take the free gift of the water of life. Taken as a whole, the bride of Christ—the church—also gives out that call. But each of us individually ("him who hears" what Jesus says about eternal life) is also to invite others to partake of the water of life.

And it's not a bad message to be sharing with our family, friends, and acquaintances, is it?

You're hurting? Come to the one who mends broken hearts. You don't see a point to your existence? Come to the one who can make sense of it all. You see something in Christians that you'd like to have for yourself? Come to Him who will make you a part of His family.

Come!

Lord, open an opportunity before me soon, even this very day, to give another Your invitation to come to You. In the name of Jesus I pray. Amen.

Practical Polytheism

They worshiped the LORD, but they also served their own gods in accordance with the customs of the nations from which they had been brought (2 Kings 17:33).

Scripture: 2 Kings 17:26-34
Song: "Jesus Calls Us"

Succoth-benoth was a deity whose name implies that women were forced into prostitution as a part of this deity's worship. Nergal was a god who presided over the underworld. Ashima was a goddess of fate. Nibhaz was an idol of an evil spirit represented as a dog. Tartak was a prince of darkness. Moloch was a god to whom children were sacrificed by throwing them into a fire. All these gods were worshiped in northern Israel by settlers brought in by the Assyrians. And all of them were worshiped right alongside Yahweh, the God of Israel.

Chilling to think of, isn't it? How could people worship such gods? And how could they mix up foreign worship like that with worship of the one true God?

But wait. What about we who like to think of our faith in Jesus as being pure? Could some of us be worshiping the god Consumerism, making our offerings at his temple—the shopping mall? Or could some of us be worshiping the deity Romance, putting a relationship above all else? or how about the idol My Political Position? or The Latest Technological Marvel? or Looking Cool? or Sports? or Sex? or . . .

You alone are Lord, **my God**. If anything else ever threatens to take the preeminent place in my life, please lead me to make it no more a priority than it deserves. In the name of Jesus, Lord and Savior of all, I pray. Amen.

Let's Debate . . . or Not

Our fathers worshiped on this mountain, but you Jews claim that the place where we must worship is in Jerusalem (John 4:20).

Scripture: John 4:16-22
Song: "Trust and Obey"

Novelist Ted Dekker wanted to see if the message of the Good Samaritan parable—love your enemies and do good to them—is alive today or not. So he went to the Middle East and discussed it with representatives of groups many Americans would consider our ideological enemies, including Hezbollah in Lebanon and Hamas in the West Bank. Writing about his journey in a book called *Tea with Hezbollah*, Dekker concludes that Jesus' teaching about love has about as much currency in the Middle East as it does with many Americans; namely, far too little.

Dekker finished his journey in northern Israel by meeting with actual Samaritans. If anybody should retain the parable's message, it should be they, right? What Dekker found, though, is that the members of this tiny surviving sect are still taken up with the doctrinal distinctions between them and Judaism.

That's exactly what happened in Jesus' interchange with the Samaritan woman at the well: she brought up those same religious differences. This might well serve to remind us of the folly of getting sidetracked by secondary issues when the supreme calling of loving God and loving others lies before us. What we need is a flow of living water, not a tempest in a teacup.

When You're dealing with my heart, **Lord,** may I never try to put You off with an argument. In the name of Jesus I pray. Amen.

Inarguable

Many of the Samaritans from that town believed in him because of the woman's testimony, "He told me everything I ever did" (John 4:39).

Scripture: John 4:35-42
Song: "Keep Telling It"

Evangelist Nicky Cruz was invited to an El Salvador prison that held some of the nation's worst criminals. In a part of the compound where not even the guards would go, he raised his voice and declared to the prisoners, "I'm not here to tell you that you're sinners, because you already know that. I'm just here to tell you my story. I want to tell you what Jesus has done in my life, and you decide what to do with it."

Cruz, a former New York gang leader, commented on what he did next in that prison. "I told them my testimony—stories I've shared thousands of times in my life yet never tire of telling. Because it's the most powerful tool God has given me. It's the one thing that can't be debated or ignored. You can ignore someone's opinion, but you can't argue with their story."

How about your own story of going through life with Jesus? Are you telling it to others?

Maybe some of your friends and acquaintances will eventually say along with the Samaritan villagers, "We no longer believe just because of what you said; now we have heard for ourselves, and we know that this man really is the Savior of the world" (v. 42).

Lord, I desire to share with others what You have done in my life. Use my story for their good, and I'll give You all the glory. I pray in Jesus' name. Amen.

Not in Form and Falsity

A time is coming and has now come when the true worshipers will worship the Father in spirit and truth, for they are the kind of worshipers the Father seeks (John 4:23).

Scripture: John 4:7-15, 23-26, 28-30
Song: "O Worship the King"

When it comes to types of Christian worship, there are flavors for just about every taste. Some people like an elaborate liturgy, with a fixed order, preselected Bible passages, and already written prayers. Others want to be more spontaneous, with prayers made up on the spot and singing that runs on and on. Some like to recite one of the foundational creeds of Christianity; others argue for "no creed but the Bible." Some see the sermon as the centerpiece of a worship experience; others put the Lord's Supper first. Some are somber, by turns sitting, standing, and kneeling. Others hop, shout, and raise their arms, bang tambourines, and dance up and down the aisles.

There's nothing wrong with thinking through what kind of worship we think God might prefer and what kind fits us best. But one thing we all need to do, regardless of how we worship, is to stop periodically and ask ourselves: Am I worshiping in spirit and truth rather than in form and falsity?

Speaking to the woman at the well, Jesus laid aside all formulas and places as a prerequisite for true worship. Worship can happen any time and any place—whenever we focus our adoration on God.

Lord, teach me how to let my spirit commune with Your Spirit and how to make the thoughts of my mind conform with Your eternal truth. In Jesus' name, amen.

Out of Gloom and Darkness

In that day the deaf will hear the words of the scroll, and out of gloom and darkness the eyes of the blind will see (Isaiah 29:18).

Scripture: Isaiah 29:17-21
Song: "Holy Spirit, Light Divine"

Fifteen-month-old Sydney Rose toddles all over the house but stops at the edge of the shadow that darkens the far end of the hall. She's not alone in this instinctive suspicion of dark corners. Most children fear the dark to some degree.

From conception unborn children know only darkness. Then, at the appointed time, they are drawn to the light. After experiencing the brilliance of day, vivid colors, and smiling faces, they perceive the difference between dark and light and find the latter far more desirable than the former.

Similarly, our spiritual existence begins in total darkness. Nevertheless, our instinctive yearning for deliverance from the gloom beckons us to seek the light. Sadly, counterfeit lights lure countless individuals away from the light of the world.

In Isaiah's day multitudes followed the wrong lights. Yet, at the appointed time, Jesus not only delivered the blind from physical darkness, but also through His death and resurrection, He imparts spiritual sight to all who seek His light.

Loving Father, You illuminate my path with the light of Jesus, and instantly I recognize the brilliance of Your smiling face. The promise of an existence far more desirable than this present one inspires my praise. In Jesus' name, I pray. Amen.

April 23–29. **Brenda K. Hendricks,** of Freeburg, Pennsylvania, enjoys writing and illustrating for God's glory. She is the author/illustrator of the Bumbly Bee picture books for beginning readers.

Give Light on the Earth

And God said, "Let there be lights in the expanse of the sky to separate the day from the night, and let them serve as signs to mark seasons and days and years, and let them . . . give light on the earth" (Genesis 1:14, 15).

Scripture: Genesis 1:14-19
Song: "Send the Light"

In the basement of an inner city church, a minister with the build of a grizzly bear gave the youth retreat's first presentation. When given the signal, his assistant turned off the lights. The audience sat captivated in total darkness. After a short pause, a small light flickered. The minister raised a three-inch birthday candle above his head and began to sing the familiar tune, "This Little Light of Mine." As strong as that man appeared, he had no power within himself to dissipate the darkness. However, the night succumbed to the tiny light he held in his hand.

Sometimes, we may feel too insignificant to make a difference in this vast darkness we call society. And it's true. We have no power in and of ourselves to repel darkness. However, God has called us to let our light shine among the men and women of our world. The light comes not from our size or strength, but from the one who lives in us. Jesus is the light of the world.

Through Him God created all things and set them in their place for a purpose. Likewise, He stationed believers in their specific locations. And, whether we realize it or not, as His disciples we naturally give light to the earth.

Creator of all things, please allow the light of Jesus to shine through me so brilliantly that others can see the face of the one who holds me near. In His name, amen.

The Long Way Around

When Pharaoh let the people go, God did not lead them on the road through the Philistine country, though that was shorter. For God said, "If they face war, they might change their minds and return to Egypt" (Exodus 13:17).

Scripture: Exodus 13:17-22
Song: "Turn Your Eyes upon Jesus"

When you're traveling through my hometown and in need of directions, be careful who you ask. A certain woman residing on Market Street (me!) has a tendency to lead people astray. But I have a good excuse. Three towns in our vicinity coexist with the same first name, ending in "town," "burg," or "ville." Sometimes I confuse those towns and blurt out "west" when I should have said "east." I can only hope that those who have been misguided will finally resort to their trusty GPS.

In an attempt to soothe my guilt after such encounters, I've convinced myself that God must have had good reason to prompt travelers to ask a blonde for directions, knowing that I'd send them the long way around. After all, God has been known to redirect people like that, taking them a farther distance than seemingly necessary. Look at the long hike He gave the Israelites on their way to Mt. Sinai. In doing so, He spared them the agony of facing battles for which they were unprepared.

As with the ancient Hebrews, God knows the battles that lie ahead of us. No doubt He often steers us from harm's way until we're better equipped to endure.

Father, when it seems You are taking me the long way around, help me to keep my eyes on Jesus. Keep me trusting in Your protective care. In Jesus' name, amen.

Blinded by Self-preservation

His parents said this because they were afraid of the Jews, for already the Jews had decided that anyone who acknowledged that Jesus was the Christ would be put out of the synagogue (John 9:22).

Scripture: John 9:18-23
Song: "I Am Resolved"

As the youngest child in our family, I was often left "holding the bag" when my siblings passed on the blame by playing the "Ask Him/Her" game. Most of the time, when I'd point out the culprit, my siblings would accuse me of tattling. Go figure. Knowing I hadn't participated in the naughtiness, did they really expect me to take the heat?

Few people willingly accept punishment for wrongs they haven't committed. But for the parents of the blind man, the threat of excommunication compelled them to turn the Pharisees' attention back to their now-seeing son. However, consider the consequence of their desire for self-preservation: Their refusal to admit the truth apparently kept them blinded to the Truth.

To some degree we have all yielded to self-preservation and have chosen the lesser of, perhaps, two evils. When given a choice, it's the natural thing to do. Nevertheless, the easier way out can blind us to a needed lesson. Even if standing firm in our faith leads to severe consequences, it can result in a closer relationship with God.

Heavenly Father, before I buckle beneath any pressure that could cause me to deny You, may Your Holy Spirit strengthen me. Through Christ I pray. Amen.

Blinded by Pride

To this they replied, "You were steeped in sin at birth; how dare you lecture us!" And they threw him out (John 9:34).

Scripture: John 9:24-34
Song: "Break Thou the Bread of Life"

During the mating season, whitetail bucks are so distracted that they barely eat. One buck challenges another to gain the "breeding rights" with any doe in the area. Usually, it only takes a few snorts and head butts to send the weaker deer on his way. However, when neither concedes to the other, the battle continues and, occasionally, the two deer lock horns. At that moment, they are both doomed to a slow, agonizing death largely due to their already malnourished condition.

Religious prestige governed the Pharisees to the point of spiritual malnutrition—they neglected to "feast" on the Word of God. When challenged by the truth of Jesus Christ, they refused to concede, professing to be followers of Moses. At that point, they had "locked horns" with pride, which blinded them to their spiritual malnutrition. Did they not seal their own fate at that point?

Sadly, many people in today's churches follow a similar path, relying on their good works to get them to Heaven. While faith without works is dead, we do good works because of our gratitude for the gracious salvation freely given from our Lord. And as we continue to partake of the bread of life, He frees us from every dangerous preoccupation.

Heavenly Father, when I "lock horns" with pride, open my eyes and set me free to "feast" on the bread of life. In the name of Christ I pray. Amen.

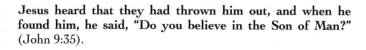

Lost and Found

Jesus heard that they had thrown him out, and when he found him, he said, "Do you believe in the Son of Man?" (John 9:35).

Scripture: John 9:35-41
Song: "When We See Christ"

My husband and I drove for five hours to acquire a 1-year-old Airedale Terrier. Shortly after arriving at her new home, she ran away. As storm clouds gathered, I called her name and searched the neighborhood for her. By the time I found the bewildered dog, she was drenched, trembling beneath a pine tree.

Her fear subsided the moment she saw me. Though it began with a frightening experience, that day quickly became one of the best days of her life. Through that experience she learned to stay close to home.

For the man in today's Scripture, the best day of his life quickly took a turn for the worse. Born blind, he received his physical sight. His countrymen should have celebrated with him. Instead, an emotional storm brewed as his parents forsook him and the Pharisees interrogated, ridiculed, and eventually excommunicated him. Imagine his bewilderment. Nevertheless, Jesus saw the "storm" approaching for the man He had healed physically. The Lord searched for him and offered him spiritual sight as well.

Jesus is always ready to accept and comfort us. No storm is so great that He can't calm it, no blindness that He cannot heal.

Dear God, when the good times turn to bad and I become confused and frightened, remind me to look up. Jesus is seeking to embrace me. In His name I pray. Amen.

All for God's Glory

"Neither this man nor his parents sinned," said Jesus, "but this happened so that the work of God might be displayed in his life" (John 9:3).

Scripture: John 9:1-17
Song: "To God Be the Glory"

"What have I done to deserve this?" The question wasn't meant to be cynical or rebellious. I sincerely wanted to know why God had led me into a fearful wilderness. I had heard people implying that sin often contributed to those kinds of "field trips." So I asked God to reveal any hidden sin in my life that I might confess it. The only response I received was, "Follow me and trust."

Although I now realize that He was always by my side, I walked in that dark tunnel for several years, rarely sensing God's presence. Occasionally, I sensed Him questioning my faith, my motives, my loyalty, my love, and my trust. But the trial was never about sin.

Throughout life we seek answers to our difficult circumstances such as depression, disease, divorce, and the death of a loved one. And we tend to blame sin for a great deal of it. Yet Jesus declared that not every tribulation results from a violation of God's will. In good times and bad, depending on how we respond, God's sterling character can shine through us. And that will certainly display the work of God in our lives.

Heavenly Father, as You teach me kingdom lessons and prepare me for my earthly work, help me to bring You glory, especially during the darkest of moments. In the holy name of Jesus, my Lord and Savior, I pray. Amen.

Grateful for the Help?

After the people saw the miraculous sign that Jesus did, they began to say, "Surely this is the Prophet who is come into the world" (John 6:14).

Scripture: John 6:1-15
Song: "Open Our Eyes, Lord"

"What are your most pressing needs?" asked a fellow church member. I was a single mom earning a small income, and I'd been praying to God about more than one need.

My cheeks turned pink, and my pulse quickened. I answered that my children could use winter coats. It hurt my pride that I couldn't meet their need on my own. But I had to recognize that I needed help.

A couple of weeks later, a couple smiled as they handed me coats for my kids. Over the next few years, I prayed to God frequently when I couldn't pay for legitimate needs. We received motor oil, gas money, grocery money, clothing, and even a car at just the right times. God's grace flowed abundantly through the love of His people, and I praised Him privately and publicly.

Sometimes I miss those days. I'm no longer poor, and I'm no longer so easily moved to joy at the simple blessings from God's hand. I would like to have more of the amazement, the deep gratitude that must have filled those hungry people as they feasted on plentiful bread and fish.

Father, You graciously meet my needs on a daily basis. Please give me the eyes to see your activity in my life and to be ever grateful. In the name of Jesus, amen.

April 30. **Tanya T. Warrington** is a freelance writer and novelist living in Masonville, Colorado. When she isn't writing, Tanya enjoys gardening, hiking, and reading.

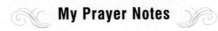

My Prayer Notes

DEVOTIONS®

MAY

"The work of God is this: to believe in the one he has sent."

—*John 6:29*

Gary Allen, Editor   **Margaret Williams,** Project Editor   Photo by Jupiterimages/Comstock/Thinkstock®

DEVOTIONS® is published quarterly by Standard Publishing, Cincinnati, Ohio, www.standardpub.com.
© 2011 by Standard Publishing. All rights reserved. Topics based on the Home Daily Bible Readings,
International Sunday School Lessons. © 2008 by the Committee on the Uniform Series. Printed in
the U.S.A. All Scripture quotations, unless otherwise indicated, are taken from the *HOLY BIBLE, NEW
INTERNATIONAL VERSION®. NIV®.* Copyright © 1973, 1978, 1984 by Biblica Inc.™ Used by
permission of Zondervan. All rights reserved. *New American Standard Bible* (NASB), © The
Lockman Foundation, 1960, 1962, 1963, 1968, 1971, 1972, 1973, 1975, 1977, 1995. *King James Version*
(KJV),* public domain.

Childlike Faith

He said to them, "It is I; don't be afraid" (John 6:20).

Scripture: John 6:16-21
Song: "Abide with Me"

One of our children was terrified by storms, another by darkness, and another by spiders. No amount of rational explanations about these things seemed to calm them. Pep talks didn't work. And being told "you're big and strong" doesn't help when you are feeling pretty small.

What our children *did* respond to, even in their worst moments of terror, was hearing: "It's OK, I'm right here with you." They implicitly believed that adults could handle anything. We were bigger and stronger than anything that might harm them.

When we grown-ups are frightened (by adult concerns, such as economic woes, cancer threats, or oil spills), reason and pep talks don't typically calm us either, do they?

But perhaps we adults could grow in our ability to trust as a child does. We could remember in our most frightening moments that we have an ever-present Savior who really can deliver us from anything. We can listen for His reassuring voice.

Life isn't easy, and the frightening moments and hours will come. We can count on it—and we can trust in Jesus Christ. We can release our fear and let our eyes focus, not on what frightens us, but rather on our mighty God.

Lord, I want to trust You in even the most frightening of circumstances. You are Lord over all lords and King above all kings. All glory to You, in Jesus' name. Amen.

May 1–May 6. **Tanya T. Warrington** is a freelance writer and novelist living in Colorado. When she isn't writing, Tanya enjoys gardening, hiking, and reading.

Grab On!

As I told you, you have seen me and still you do not believe (John 6:36).

Scripture: John 6:36-40
Song: "The Lifeboat"

In lifeguard training I learned that drowning victims can become so panicked that they'll grab their would-be rescuers in a death grip. As a result, the trainer emphasized that lifeguards must exhaust all land-rescue options before diving into the water to save someone. We were taught to throw out a buoy, reach with a hooked pole, or find something else to extend to the struggling swimmer. Even this strategy can go awry, however, if the drowning person is too frightened to listen to directions. He or she can stare right at the rescue tool, but not put any trust in its ability to help. If the victim won't grab onto the extended object, she or he may drown with rescue within reach.

The word translated "seen" in this verse means "stared at or perceived the details of." Some people stared at Jesus, studying details about Him, but they did not trust Him implicitly. They didn't recognize Him as the Son of God and as their personal deliverer.

May we spend the time to get to know Jesus well. He loves us and promises to be with us no matter how chaotic or turbulent the waters of our life may be.

Lord, I'm sitting at Your feet, eager to know You. I want to understand as much as I can about Your heart and Your will. I want to work and rest with You. I want to be Your disciple, learning from You and serving You, today and every day. In the name of Jesus I pray. Amen.

A Better Future Awaits

I tell you the truth, he who believes has everlasting life (John 6:47).

Scripture: John 6:41-51
Song: "How Beautiful Heaven Must Be"

Some days, everlasting life doesn't feel like a gift. When I focus on my difficulties, life can seem too long. Yesterday was one of those days. My head hurt, and my body ached. It was also a day of forgetting things. Not a horrible day, but an irritating one.

By late afternoon, I needed refreshment. So I transplanted several plants and enjoyed the greenery, the feel of soil on my hands. Then I noticed the mess that I'd made. One thing led to another, and I dug into cleaning our home. It felt good. But when my husband came home, I discovered I hadn't begun dinner preparations.

My understanding husband took us out to dinner. Spending time together was great. It changed my whole perspective about my day.

The same shift in perspective happens when I focus on everlasting life with Him. Little daily trials become more livable when I remember that He is with me always. The big trials become more manageable when I remember that they are temporary. Our forever home is ahead. Just imagine!

Thank You, **Jesus**, for the everlasting home that You are preparing for me. It is difficult for me to comprehend eternity, but I look forward to seeing You face-to-face. Help me to remember daily that Heaven waits, so that I will handle future hardships with faith, patience, and courage. Through Christ I pray. Amen.

The Only Fuel

The Spirit gives life; the flesh counts for nothing (John 6:63).

Scripture: John 6:60-65
Song: "Spirit of the Living God"

By the time I was done shoveling snow, I was running late for Bible study. On the way my car suddenly slowed down of its own accord. That's when I remembered: The fuel gauge had hit empty the night before. A gas station was close, though, so I coasted, making it to the station's driveway—which was an icy, steep hill. I held my breath and prayed. Two-thirds of the way up, the car went dead. No amount of pleading or urging would get it going again.

I wish I could say that I shouted for help. I got out of the car, however, put it in neutral, and pushed as hard as I could. The car barely moved. I gave it another try. It moved forward maybe a few inches and then began sliding backwards. My two children were in the car! I scrambled for footing and shoved my right foot onto the emergency brake. Thanks be to God, the car stopped.

We too need fuel to keep on functioning. For our physical self air, water, and food are must-haves. For our spiritual self, only the Holy Spirit gives us life. Our own efforts cannot fill us with the living God's presence, no matter how much we try. Only the Spirit will do.

Thank You for the gift of the Holy Spirit, **Lord.** When I was dead in my sins, You rescued me and gave me new life. Help me to stop trying to earn what You've already given me without any strings attached. In the name of Jesus I pray. Amen.

Let's Keep Following Him

From this time many of his disciples turned back and no longer followed him (John 6:66).

Scripture: John 6:66-71
Song: "What a Friend We Have in Jesus"

The kids were full of energy as we began hiking up the trail. Our most active child started running, and the other four raced to catch up. My husband and I laughed. They had never backpacked before and couldn't wait for the adventure. "Let's see what their pace is after a few miles," my husband said.

The trail wound ever upward. When we'd barely gotten started, we paused by a pond and half the kids voted that we'd gone far enough. Further on, we heard much more grumbling . . .

We encouraged the kids to keep walking. When we'd trekked half of the planned distance, carrying packs no longer appealed to any of them. We only hiked another 10 minutes before we parents decided that this day had been long enough. Cheers sounded as we lowered our packs to the ground.

How often do we modern followers of Christ feel tempted to call the Christian journey finished? Especially when the way is rougher than we first thought? Sometimes the way seems impossibly steep when we're under a heavy burden. Other times the weight of trials seems like an impossible load. And yet when we walk with God, trusting Him the best we can, His strength and peace make the impossible possible.

I'm just a weak human being, **Lord,** but I give You my whole heart. Lead me where You will. I will follow by Your grace and in Your strength. I know that You know where we are going, and that is enough. In Christ I pray. Amen.

Trust Walk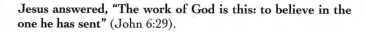

Jesus answered, "The work of God is this: to believe in the one he has sent" (John 6:29).

Scripture: John 6:22-35
Song: "Living by Faith"

At church camp I was told to close my eyes and let my partner lead me. That was it? It didn't sound like much of a challenge; that is, until the game began. Almost immediately she forgot to warn me about a tree stump, and I hit my leg against it. If my friend could miss something that big, what else might she do? What other injuries might I incur?

I found myself trying to peep under the bandana to double-check where my feet were going. I couldn't see much of anything, but I felt slightly more in control. Who would have guessed that trust in my best buddy's care would disappear so quickly?

These days I find myself on a much longer "trust walk" with a friend I can't even see. I'm often in the dark about where the journey is going, but God leads me perfectly. He knows just when to urge me on and when to lead without words. Jesus lets me know when I am straying off course and encourages me with words of comfort when I am scared. I continue to learn daily how to fully trust in Him who is most trustworthy.

Trusting isn't always easy, **Heavenly Father,** but You help me to keep discovering how good You are. You watch over me and tenderly take care of my soul. With You as my Shepherd, I know that I am in the best of hands. Lead on, I will follow. But please don't go too fast! In the name of Jesus, who lives and reigns with You and the Holy Spirit, one God, now and forever, amen.

He Advised the Unpopular

The messenger . . . spoke to [Micaiah] saying, "Behold, the words of the prophets are uniformly favorable to the king. So please let your word be like one of them and speak favorably" (2 Chronicles 18:12, *New American Standard Bible*).

Scripture: 2 Chronicles 18:12-20
Song: "How Gentle God's Commands"

When Sara's husband drank, he physically abused her, terrifying their three children. Sara's minister advised her to leave her husband because she was in danger. Reluctantly, she left and later divorced him. About this same time my friend, Peter, dedicated his life to Christ, though his wife wanted nothing to do with God.

Peter met Sara in church when they were both extremely vulnerable. They soon felt they'd fallen in love. Peter wanted to divorce his wife and marry Sara, but his minister advised the difficult and unpopular: wait, trust God for his own wife's salvation.

Peter really didn't want to hear such counsel! After they married, Peter and Sara frequently quarreled with their stepchildren, and there was constant turmoil with the ex-spouses. The two families never did become one.

God's instructions may seem difficult for a season—and hard to speak to others, as the prophet Micaiah knew. But if we follow His plan for our lives, we will know His peace.

Dear Lord, please give me grace to speak Your truth and obey Your counsel, even when it is difficult or unpopular. In Jesus' name I pray, amen.

May 7–13. **Marty Prudhomme,** of Mandeville, Louisiana, is a great grandmother who teaches Bible studies and leads a friendship-evangelism ministry called Adopt a Block.

He Anoints the Called

Have him stand before Eleazar the priest and before all the congregation, and commission him in their sight (Numbers 27:19, *New American Standard Bible*).

Scripture: Numbers 27:12-20
Song: "The Spirit of the Lord Is Upon Me"

There are so many hurting women in the community, even in the church, who need healing from their emotional wounds. My church leaders recognized God was calling me to minister to such women. They laid hands on me, praying that the Lord would commission and anoint me for women's ministry.

God began giving me creative ideas about how to proceed. He seemed to give me wisdom in counseling and taught me what to pray. Often, in the middle of the night, I'd awaken with ideas that would minister to women. (I began keeping a notepad on my nightstand so I could jot these insights.) I believe the prayers of my church elders were the beginning of a new calling on my life.

Similarly, Moses brought Joshua before the people and their priest so that Joshua could be publicly commissioned for leadership. There is something of crucial importance to such an act. It tells the whole gathered community that it is God who calls and God who empowers so that His kingdom work may be carried out effectively. I'm so grateful God still anoints and equips His children to minister.

Father, You are wondrous and wonderful in all Your ways. Thank You for continuing to use ordinary men and women to do extraordinary tasks. Please guide me and give me increasing wisdom for my ministry among Your people. In Jesus' name, amen.

God Chooses the Humble

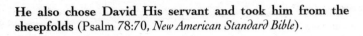

He also chose David His servant and took him from the sheepfolds (Psalm 78:70, *New American Standard Bible*).

Scripture: Psalm 78:67-72
Song: "Here Am I Lord; Send Me"

My friend Gail grew up in a farming community in Oregon. Much of her childhood was spent working to bring in the crops at harvest time. In fact, each summer she spent her school vacation working in the fields. No one could have possibly guessed this rosy-cheeked child would become an evangelist, international missionary, and teacher of God's Word. No one knew she would be a counselor to ministers from all over the world.

The only clue to Gail's future was that she clearly loved the Lord. One summer the missionary that visited Gail's church touched her heart. Gail immediately felt a strong desire to tell others about God's gift of salvation through Jesus Christ. God called, and Gail answered, "Yes, Lord, I'll go for You."

The Lord took a little farm girl and prepared her to travel the world as His ambassador. Gail delights in sharing the gospel, seeing people healed and set free from sin's bondage.

We may think we cannot do anything great for the Lord. But when He calls us, He equips us. God seldom chooses the great and the mighty; He chooses the humble and the willing, like King David.

Dear Lord, You took me, a poor barefoot child, who lived on a street made of clam shells, and set my feet upon the Solid Rock, Christ Jesus. You brought me up from the pit and called me to be Your daughter. Help me, Lord, to always answer Your call and to obey Your will. In Jesus' name I pray.

For the Defense: God!

The LORD is their strength, and He is a saving defense to His anointed (Psalm 28:8, *New American Standard Bible*).

Scripture: Psalm 28
Song: "He Is My Defense"

It was a dark day when my husband, Bill, came home from work and announced, "We are being sued for a million dollars." Previously Bill told me about an employee who had been neglecting his work. The man continually caused difficulties among his coworkers. Bill warned the fellow several times about his poor work habits and agonized over whether to fire this man. Eventually, Bill had no choice. Now the man was out for vengeance.

After the initial shock, we turned to the Lord, searching the Scriptures for encouragement. "Help, Lord," was our cry. "This situation is so far beyond our control; we have nowhere else to turn, and no money to fight this. Our trust is in You." The Lord assured us He was our defense.

After months of waiting for a preliminary hearing, the case finally went to the judge. He threw it out of court; the case never went to trial. Later we learned that Bill's ex-employee had tried to sue other employers in the past.

I still believe that God was our defense attorney throughout this ordeal. When we cried out to the Lord, He heard from Heaven, gave us strength to face this trial, and delivered us.

Dear Lord, thank You for coming to my defense when I am surrounded by danger. Keep growing my confidence in You as we deepen our relationship. You are strong when I am weak, and for that I am so grateful. Praise You, Lord Jesus! Amen.

Shine Thy Face upon Me

O God of hosts, restore us, and cause Your face to shine upon us, and we will be saved (Psalm 80:7, *New American Standard Bible*).

Scripture: Psalm 80:1-7
Song: "Go and Sin No More"

One summer all three of our children moved out of the house within the same week. Our son went to Kuwait for Desert Storm, one daughter got married and moved away, and the other went to the Philippines to be a missionary. Suddenly, I became unreasonably angry with my husband, Bill. I blamed him for every mistake he ever made with our children (and, believe me, I could remember them all).

I never thought the empty-nest syndrome would bother me. But now I could feel the irritation rising up inside, and I complained about everything. Anger became my enemy, robbing me of peace and stealing my joy.

Then I prayed, "Lord, I don't want to be angry any more. I am being completely unreasonable. Bill hasn't changed—I have." After many tears of repentance, I asked the Lord, "Please forgive me and deliver me from this unreasonable rage. Restore the joy of my salvation, Lord. Change me, even if my circumstances never change."

I recognized my sin, sincerely repented, and the anger left me. Suddenly I knew what it meant to sense the Lord's face shining on me. He restored my peace and filled me with joy.

Dear Lord, when I call, You hear my prayer and save me from destruction. Build Your character within me. Help me to walk in the Spirit and not in the flesh. Amen.

No Confusion

A stranger they simply will not follow, but will flee from him, because they do not know the voice of strangers (John 10:5, *New American Standard Bible*).

Scripture: John 10:1-6
Song: "My Sheep Know My Voice"

A degenerative eye disease robbed my friend Marilee of her sight several years ago. For the first few years, her husband helped her cope with the challenges of blindness. But when he passed away, Marilee felt lost. Yet she decided to stay in the house they had lived in for all their married life.

It has not been easy for Marilee to live alone. She needed special organizing in the house, especially in the kitchen. And she required a phone set-up made specifically for the blind.

One skill she quickly learned: to recognize her friend's voices, the unique sound of each. But last week, at a Christian ladies meeting, someone came up to Marilee asking how she was doing. She quickly reached out to touch the lady and asked, "Who is this?" The lady recognized Marilee, but Marilee did not know her. And I could see a look of bewilderment on Marilee's face. She knew her friends, but a stranger's voice brought confusion.

This is how we are to recognize our Shepherd's voice. No matter how many voices surround us, we should immediately distinguish His voice. And that voice will never cause confusion.

Dear Lord, teach this sheep to hear and follow Your voice. There are so many voices that vie for my attention, but I want to recognize You at all times. Help me to distinguish between my own desires (that seem to speak so loudly) and Your good and perfect will. Through Christ I pray. Amen.

◈ **Come In!** ◈

I am the door, if anyone enters through Me, he will be saved, and will go in and out and find pasture (John 10:9, *New American Standard Bible*).

Scripture: John 10:7-18
Song: "The Shepherd Is the Lamb"

When I was a child, my family never locked the front door of our house. Dad lost the key shortly after we moved in and didn't bother to make another one. And that was perfectly safe in our semirural area of New Orleans, where everyone knew each other so well.

I came and went as I pleased. Neither did it occur to me to knock on the door when I came home from school. I just walked in without giving it a thought. It was my house, and I felt perfectly safe. Even when the family drove off to Grandma's on vacation, the front door remained unlocked. After all, no one would ever bother to rob our family!

When I became a Christian, I discovered that only one door led into God's kingdom. I had no problem relating to His "open door policy." I was the sheep of His pasture, who freely walked through His front door, feeling protected and at home.

Jesus is the door by which every one of us must enter. He is the Shepherd of every willing soul, everyone who desires to be a sheep of His pasture.

O Eternal Lord God, thank You for inviting me into Your pasture. The door was unlocked so I could freely enter, and I felt safe walking right in. Please keep this sheep from wondering into another pasture. In the name of the Father, the Son, and the Holy Spirit, I pray. Amen.

The Real Winner

I count all things but loss for the excellency of the knowledge of Christ Jesus my Lord: for whom I have suffered the loss of all things, and do count them but dung, that I may win Christ (Philippians 3:8, *King James Version*).

Scripture: Philippians 3:7-11
Song: "I Have Decided to Follow Jesus"

Roman Emperor Joseph II said the following about his sister, Marie Antoinette: "The queen is a pretty woman, but she is empty-headed . . . and wastes her days running from dissipation to dissipation, some of which are perfectly allowable, but nonetheless dangerous, because they prevent her from having the thoughts she needs so badly."

Human nature hasn't changed much over the centuries. These words could easily apply to any rich, spoiled celebrity in modern America. Rarely are wealth and wisdom possessed by the same person. But fame and foolishness often go together.

Marie Antoinette wore herself out gadding about, partying hard, and behaving badly. The more money she spent, the more she impoverished her mind. There's no wisdom in the palace, but look what we find in a prison. The apostle Paul sat in a stinking cell, poor, hungry, and cut off from society. Nonetheless he enjoyed his own El Dorado. The treasures of Christ filled his mind to overflowing. (Anything else seemed like garbage.)

Father, help me to spend my time in learning and living Your Word. Keep me from the vanity that would make me a loser in your eyes. In Jesus' name I pray. Amen.

May 14–20. **Richard Robinson** is a minister and the teacher on the radio program, "Holy Ground," in Denver, Colorado. He enjoys singing, writing, and doing computer graphic design.

The Greatest Marvel

For the Father loveth the Son, and sheweth him all things that himself doeth: and he will shew him greater works than these, that ye may marvel (John 5:20, *King James Version*).

Scripture: John 5:19-24
Song: "Lord, I Need You"

There once lived a family of mice in the body of an old grand piano. From their ebony box, they heard the most beautiful music and became very curious about its origin. One day, one of them scampered into the sound case and discovered long cables all lined up in a row, vibrating. The mystery was finally solved.

However, one day another mouse discovered a set of hammers striking the cables. Surely this was a deeper discovery! With a sense of great enlightenment, they counted and measured the hammers, noted their shape, color, and motion. But they never did perceive the powerful, graceful fingers of the master pianist prsessing the keys.

This is the tale of mice and men, for within this earthly life the divine Master skillfully plays—so often undetected. Jesus, of course, saw what His heavenly Father was doing, and, like Jesus, we need to see the Father's hands at work in the world. And like Jesus, the more we see God at work, the more we can glorify Him and cooperate with what He is doing. In the end, the greatest marvel is the God behind it all.

Creator of Heaven and earth, open my eyes to discover Your hand in both the world at large and in my own life. May I never rob You of Your glory by focusing on secondary causes. In the holy name of Jesus, my Lord and Savior, I pray. Amen.

Booing the Judge

And hath given him authority to execute judgment also, because he is the Son of man (John 5:27, *King James Version*).

Scripture: John 5:25-29
Song: "Cleanse Me"

Today Jesus is, for the most part, well thought of. He is admired as a teacher, a prophet, and a guru who opens up divine reality for us. But He is not so widely believed to be the only Savior and judge of the world. If you were on a television talk show and said, "Jesus has changed my life," the crowd would cheer. But if you were to say, "We can't be forgiven, or come to know God, except through Jesus," you would be booed. In a pluralistic society, one Savior from one book teaching one way to Heaven will be considered "narrow-minded."

Where has this led us? For half a century, Americans have worshiped at the altar of positive thinking and sacrificed to the god of moral relativism. These highly subjective philosophies deny the elephant in the room—mankind's sin.

In today's passage Jesus offers life (a positive) and will execute judgment (a negative). But it seems that the world will accept Him as a savior if only they can dethrone Him as a judge! Yet to receive the good news of salvation, we must be driven to it by the bad news. (In other words, there is one prime qualification for salvation: You must be a sinner.) In the meantime, Jesus is patiently wooing sinners over their booing.

Dear Jesus, I adore You in all Your roles, including judge of the universe. Help me to live in reverence of You and enjoy Your favor, until the day I stand before You. In my Savior's name I pray. Amen.

Our Shepherd's Voice

My sheep hear my voice, and I know them, and they follow me (John 10:27, *King James Version*).

Scripture: John 10:22-28
Song: "Peace, Perfect Peace"

The Middle East is the cradle of civilization, the area of the world where shepherding was first practiced as a vocation. And there are many shepherds still there today, daily leading their flocks, even in places where violent unrest frequently breaks out. Missionary Ron Jones, who serves with the Christian and Missionary Alliance in Israel, wrote this in his prayer letter:

"Yesterday, a friend shared with us something she observed that was a delightful reminder of God's care for us. She watched a shepherd caring for his flock near an area where guns are fired. Every time the shots rang out, the sheep scattered in fright. The shepherd then touched each of them with his staff and spoke calmly to them, and the sheep settled down immediately because they trusted the shepherd. And then another shot sounded, and the same routine unfolded again. Each time, the sheep needed the shepherd to orient them again and to reassure them they were safe."

If natural shepherds can calm sheep startled by gunfire, what can our heavenly Shepherd do? In fact, Judaism and the Roman Empire together never could drown out the reassuring voice of Jesus. That same voice not only calls but also calms.

Dear Lord Jesus, keep me close to Your side that I may always hear Your loving voice. When danger is near, be nearer to calm my fears. In the name of the Father, the Son, and the Holy Spirit, I pray. Amen.

Flies on the Track?

Then after that saith he to his disciples, Let us go into Judaea again (John 11:7, *King James Version*).

Scripture: John 11:1-10
Song: "Guide Me, O Thou Great Jehovah"

As reported in the *Ottawa Citizen,* a Canadian train in the nineteenth century ran into a sea of flies about 20 miles out of Cornwall. The train, impervious to the mass of insects, plowed through the flies at a mile a minute for several miles. At one point, the train stopped to clean off the track to free the wheels, then was on its way again.

On arrival at Montreal, the engine presented a truly bizarre spectacle. The bars of the cowcatcher were filled right up with flies. The front of the engine was plastered several inches thick. The little critters were ground into mush in the driving rod. They were in everything. But the locomotive won the battle against an innumerable host and trampled on them all!

When Jesus told His disciples of His decision to go back into Judaea (v. 7), the disciples were surprised. "Master, the Jews of late sought to stone thee; and goest thou thither again?" (v. 8). Jesus reminded them that the real danger was in *avoiding* the Father's will, which would lead to stumbling in the dark (v. 9).

Like Jesus, we must never get sidetracked, much less derailed, in pursuing the Father's will. Those who oppose us may swarm like flies, but the will of God is an unstoppable iron horse.

Dear Heavenly Father, be the strength of my life, especially as I seek to follow Your will. I know there's no turning back, so give me the momentum to overcome all obstacles in my way. For Jesus' sake I pray. Amen.

Sifted by Delay

**Then said Jesus unto them plainly, Lazarus is dead.
And I am glad for your sakes that I was not there, to the
intent ye may believe; nevertheless let us go unto him** (John
11:14, 15, *King James Version*).

Scripture: John 11:11-16
Song: "Wait on the Lord"

Which is safer: Traveling in a rocket ship at Mach 20 in outer
space or traveling 20 miles per hour going to the corner grocery store? From our perspective, a car seems much safer. From
God's perspective, they are the same. Faith is simply operating
from God's point of view.

Like wheat and chaff piled together, the best saints are a curious mixture of faith and unbelief. In today's passage Jesus
winnowed the chaff by purposely staying away from Bethany
until Lazarus died (vv. 11-14). In fact, Jesus was "glad" that He
could focus on what He alone could do.

When Lazarus died, all other measures outside of Jesus be-
came meaningless, and the disciples were bracing for the worst.
Thomas spoke for them all when he said with a fatalistic loyalty,
"Let us also go, that we may die with him" (see v. 16).

Jesus was going to perform a resurrection; they thought they
were going to their execution! But let us remember: we can expect the unexpected with Jesus. And a delay may mean that
God is simply sifting the wheat.

Father in Heaven, help me to wait upon You with full assurance today. May Your
grace make me both loyal and optimistic as Your marvelous plans unfold. In the
name of Your Son, my Savior, I pray. Amen.

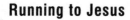

Running to Jesus

Then Martha, as soon as she heard that Jesus was coming, went and met him: but Mary sat still in the house (John 11:20, *King James Version*).

Scripture: John 11:17-27, 41-44
Song: "Come with Your Heartache"

The events surrounding Lazarus' resurrection reveal the strengths and weaknesses of his two sisters. The death in the family drew together many neighbors and friends to comfort the two women. As Jesus entered Bethany, Martha immediately left their house to go meet him. However, Mary chose to remain in the house. Nineteenth-century Bible commentator J. C. Ryle drew valuable lessons from this contrast:

"Martha—active, stirring, busy, demonstrative, cannot wait, but runs impulsively to meet Jesus.

"Mary—quiet, gentle, pensive, contemplative, meek, sits passively at home. Yet I venture to think that of the two sisters, Martha here appears to most advantage."

By not stirring Mary certainly missed hearing our Lord's glorious declaration about himself. Yet on a former occasion, the passive Mary showed more grace than the active Martha (see Luke 10:38-42). But this time, Martha is to be commended.

Depending on the circumstances, our natural temperament can be an asset or a liability. Even the best disciples can become victims of their own flawed personalities.

Father, You know my every weakness and strength. When I feel lonely, bring me out of my isolation to receive Your comfort. When I'm afraid, pull me close and give me the courage to meet the challenge. In Christ's precious name I pray. Amen.

Need a Little Help?

You and these people who come to you will only wear your-selves out. The work is too heavy for you; you cannot handle it alone (Exodus 18:18).

Scripture: Exodus 18:13-23
Song: "O God, the Help of All Thy Saints"

My mother proudly presented me with a homemade apple cobbler, one of my favorites. I was amazed that this elderly, arthritic woman could produce such a delicious dessert. As we enjoyed the sugary, cinnamon treat, I asked her how she'd managed to get it done.

"Well," she admitted, "I had a little help. Ruth was here to clean, so she peeled and cut up the apples. Then after I measured the crust ingredients, Sue came, and I asked her to mix it for me and roll it out. And then Donald was here for supper, so he put it in the oven for me and took it out when it was ready."

She looked at me with a sly grin. "I knew I could bake you a cobbler if I put my mind to it!"

This woman of God did not need the advice Jethro gave Moses—she lived it. Throughout my life I saw that she was a master of delegation, from rounding up stray cows to getting church dinners organized. She understood that there are things we should not attempt alone; we'll just wear ourselves out.

Heavenly Father, You have given us great tasks that are too much for us to do alone. Help us to carry out Your work by leading others to be involved as well. Help us to understand that You can use anyone to accomplish Your will. In Jesus' name, amen.

May 21–27. **Lanita Bradley** is a worker for Christ, a writer, wife, mother, grandmother, and friend who lives in Fort Thomas, Kentucky.

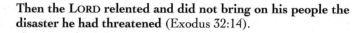

Deflating the Anger

Then the LORD relented and did not bring on his people the disaster he had threatened (Exodus 32:14).

Scripture: Exodus 32:7-14
Song: "Sweet, Sweet Spirit"

I hurried from my car into the kitchen, ready to prepare the side dishes for the meat my daughter had put in the oven when she got home from school. But the oven was cold, the roast uncooked. We would not have a hot meal ready in 20 minutes as I'd planned. I was furious! How could a 16-year-old be so irresponsible? Thankfully, my husband reached me first.

"She feels so bad about it," he said, pleadingly. "She just remembered a few minutes ago. She is so worried about what you'll say. I told her it would be OK. We'll just go to a fast food place on our way to church tonight. There's no reason to blow up at her."

His soothing words helped to drain my anger, and we had a pleasant dinner together after all. I accepted my daughter's humble apology, and all was well.

Just as Moses soothed God's anger against the Israelites, I can, with the Spirit's guidance, placate those who are upset because of another person's actions. Rather than thinking "I'll just stay out of the way" and let them work it out, I can be a peacemaker, as my husband was. Helping people avoid hurtful words can be a wonderful way to love them.

Dear God and Father, I am often disappointed in the actions of others. Please help me to hold my tongue at those times. Help me say soothing words to others when they start to say words they'll regret. In Jesus' name I pray. Amen.

The Gift of Mercy

Have mercy on me, O God, according to your unfailing love; according to your great compassion blot out my transgressions (Psalm 51:1).

Scripture: Psalm 51:1-7
Song: "Surely Goodness and Mercy"

Even as a new driver, I felt confident I could drive well in any situation. When my mother and I went shopping in a busy city, I insisted on driving. To my dismay, I soon found myself going the wrong way on a one-way street.

"Quick! Into this parking lot!" Mother said, as cars came toward us. I swerved into the lot just as the honking cars passed.

I sat there, shaken. "I am *so* sorry!" I said. "I was sure I knew where to go."

"Don't worry about it. You'll be fine now. Let's get going," she said. As I pulled back onto the street (going the right direction), I was immensely grateful for the mercy she extended to me.

And what a small matter—compared to God's mercy when I fail on a much grander scale. I neglect His Word, I say things I should not say, I ignore the needs of others, and I constantly act selfishly. As Paul said, "For what I do is not the good I want to do; no, the evil I do not want to do—this I keep on doing" (Romans 7:19). And yet I receive God's forgiveness bought for me through Christ's blood on the cross. Thanks be to God for His gift of mercy!

Almighty God, ruler of the universe, I come to You with a humble and contrite heart. I ask, as did David and Paul, that You cleanse my heart and forgive me of my sins. Renew my spirit and keep me steadfast in service. Through Christ, amen.

What Shakes You?

LORD, who may dwell in your sanctuary? Who may live on your holy hill? (Psalm 15:1).

Scripture: Psalm 15
Song: "To Love Someone More Dearly"

My friend Ruth's doctor said her cancer was out of control; it was time to call hospice. She said to me, "I feel that I'm ready. Unlike others who have no warning, I have time to hug and be hugged, to find and to throw away. I'm anticipating the promises. I've been around long enough to know that there are worse things than death." Even facing death does not shake Ruth or her faith. Her positive attitude lifts her friends and family.

What truly shakes most of us? death? job loss? illness? an endangered child? As I face my own challenges, my faith sometimes falters.

In Psalm 15 David gives a formula for dwelling with God. Being blameless is a tall order, but David defines what's involved: speaking truth, treating neighbors fairly, disdaining evil, honoring those who fear God, showing honesty in commitments, and lending money without interest. Distilling righteousness into such a short list makes it seem much more achievable.

Ruth and her husband, Bob, demonstrate these virtues in their lives. As Ruth said about Bob: "I kind of mix him up with God and Jesus, for I see them through him." What greater thing could be said about us from those who know us best?

Heavenly Father, I know that You can guide me through difficulties that shake my faith. Please show me how to treat others honestly and generously, that I may live on Your holy hill. In Jesus' name I pray. Amen.

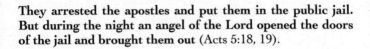

Do You Want to Be Free?

They arrested the apostles and put them in the public jail. But during the night an angel of the Lord opened the doors of the jail and brought them out (Acts 5:18, 19).

Scripture: Acts 5:17-21
Song: "There Is Power in the Blood"

Raymond Towler was given a life sentence for kidnapping and raping two teens in May of 1981. The victims said a man lured them into the woods. Recent DNA tests on the children's clothing showed he did not commit the crime, however. And after 29 years of unjust imprisonment, he was freed.

"There are a lot of things I was missing, but I have to use my faith in God to stay positive for the future," Towler said. "I do wish my parents could have seen this day—and know that I've been telling the truth for all these years."

No doubt his release after 29 years seemed almost as miraculous to Raymond Towler as did the angel's freeing the apostles when they were wrongfully imprisoned. Both were glad to get back to living out God's plan for them.

We are all imprisoned by sin and can be freed only by the blood of Jesus Christ, which has already been shed for us. Just as Raymond and the apostles accepted their opportunity for freedom, so I can gladly accept the freedom that Jesus offers me—and go into the world to live for Him.

Dear Lord of Heaven's Armies, I thank You for freeing me to live eternally with You through Jesus Your Son. Help me to break the bonds of sin, living for You and sharing with others the good news of Your saving grace. I pray this prayer in the name of Jesus, my merciful Savior and Lord. Amen.

Choosing the Right Road

Enter through the narrow gate. For wide is the gate and broad is the road that leads to destruction, and many enter through it (Matthew 7:13).

Scripture: Matthew 7:13-20
Song: "Dear Lord and Father of Mankind"

Jonathan finished college in four years with a major in social work. He now holds a responsible job working with teens in Harlem while working at night to complete his master's degree. Jonathan was identified in second grade as having a learning disability. But his determined focus on his goals helped him to overcome his handicap.

Melissa took six years to finish college, eventually receiving a liberal arts degree. She too wants to help people as a social worker. Even though she has a college diploma, however, she is not qualified for a social-work job and is unclear about her future. She would like to follow in Jonathan's steps, but Melissa has not shown the perseverance necessary to succeed.

My growth in the spiritual life can, in a sense, emulate the approach of either Jonathan or Melissa. I can stay focused on the call of God and pursue that goal single-mindedly. Or I can dabble in Christianity, sometimes trying to live for Jesus but more often thinking only of myself. The narrow road takes more effort and requires perseverance. It's the one I prefer, for I want to enter through the narrow gate that leads to eternal life.

Heavenly Father, I praise Your name for Your promise of eternal life. Please guide my life that I may stay on the narrow path and avoid the wide, easy road. May I focus on You and Your will in my life. Through Christ, amen.

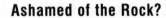

Ashamed of the Rock?

Jesus answered, "I am the way and the truth and the life. No one comes to the Father except through me" (John 14:6).

Scripture: John 14:1-14
Song: "I Love to Tell the Story"

When my 8-year-old granddaughter Kinley heard about tryouts for the public school talent show, she enthusiastically entered with a speech titled "God, My Rock." Her dad asked her why she made this unusual choice.

"So I can tell lots of people about Jesus," was the reply.

The teacher in charge, also a believer, allowed her to give her speech at the talent show. I was humbled at the thought. Would I be willing to speak in a secular situation to my peers about "God, my Rock"?

How many times do I have an opportunity to speak up for Jesus? When asked how my weekend went, do I speak of my experience at worship? When asked why I helped someone in need, do I merely say, "That's just the way I was raised," or "I enjoy helping people"?

Do we give Jesus the credit for our faithful lives . . . or avoid mentioning Him outside of Christian gatherings?

As I ponder my own daily witness, I remember that "a little child will lead them" (Isaiah 11:6). I want to follow Kinley's footsteps in openly telling others about God and His Son Jesus. He indeed is my Rock, so why should I be ashamed of Him?

Almighty Father, I am humbled by this little child's faith. I want to be more forthright in telling others about You and the difference You make in my life. Please help me to be bold in speaking for You. In Your Son's name I pray. Amen.

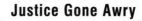

Justice Gone Awry

One witness is not enough to convict a man accused of any crime or offense he may have committed (Deuteronomy 19:15).

Scripture: Deuteronomy 19:15-20
Song: "If You will Only Let God Guide You"

My two children were fighting—again. My 5-year old daughter screamed. Her 11-year-old brother, Mark, yelled, "Stop it!"

Enough. I stormed into the room. Before I could say a word my son said, "She started it."

"Did not," Jo Anne said and stomped her foot.

"What do you want me to do?" I said to Mark. "Spank her?"

"Yup," Mark said, grinning.

"All right," I picked Jo Anne up and gave her a couple of swats. The screaming turned to crying and my heart broke. Why had I let anger overtake me?

I cuddled Jo Anne and told her I loved her and was sorry I'd gotten angry. Her sobs subsided. Peace descended on the house.

Looking back, I see how my anger and Mark's word caused Jo Anne to be spanked. The look on Mark's face told me that he should have been disciplined also. As for me, I should have investigated deeper into the real problem.

Truly, the wisdom of God is stated in Deuteronomy 19. Two witnesses are necessary for proper judgment.

Heavenly Father, I am reminded how I fail to follow Your guidance. Your wisdom makes for true justice and peace. In the love of Jesus., Amen.

May 28–31. **Elizabeth Van Liere** lives in Montrose, Colorado, and feels blessed by God to live close to the beautiful San Juan Mountains.

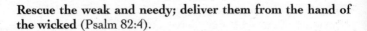

The Blessings of Persecution

Rescue the weak and needy; deliver them from the hand of the wicked (Psalm 82:4).

Scripture: Psalm 82
Song: "Rescue the Perishing"

The title of today's devotional comes from an issue of *Voice of the Martyrs* magazine. Alka, aged 20, and her grandmother, Sharma, live in India. Sharma teaches the villagers about Jesus. Their village is steeped in superstition.

Alka was raped in her village. Her grandmother said, "Alka was attacked because she teaches the gospel. The people thought this crime would make us leave, but I am staying here."

In anger the villagers locked Sharma and Alka inside their small church for five days without food or water. The two women prayed.

Voice of the Martyrs heard about the ordeal. Lawyers and volunteers came to free the women. Ministry partners now provide spiritual and legal counseling, as well as food and shelter. Sharma continues teaching about God. "I worship a living God," she says. "He will take care of us."

Another persecuted Christian put it this way: "I came away more excited about Christ. Persecution increases faith."

What can we do to help? We can pray and give. We can be God's hands. We can rescue the weak and needy and deliver them from the hands of the wicked. We can turn persecution into blessings.

Heavenly Father, would I call persecution a blessing? Let my prayers rise to You for those who daily face pain and sorrow because of their love for You. Give me a heart for all of those who suffer for the sake of Jesus. In His name, amen.

Does God Ignore Evil?

For all this, his anger is not turned away, his hand is still upraised (Isaiah 10:4).

Scripture: Isaiah 10:1-4
Song: "God Moves in a Mysterious Way"

"You are sinning," Isaiah proclaimed to the corrupt judges ruling over God's people. "God is holy and cannot look at sin. Your sin is separating you from God." How his voice must have thundered as he repeated, "God is angry! You will be punished."

As God's spokesman Isaiah threatened them: "The day of reckoning is coming. Who will help you? Where will you hide? What good will the money you have taken do you?"

The days of unjust laws, depriving the poor, and justice withheld are with us even today. Legislators make unjust laws. Words from our constitution have been misinterpreted. Our children are prohibited from praying publicly in school.

Can we sit by and do nothing? Yet we are to trust God, remembering that His kingdom is clearly not the kingdom of this world. God is merciful and He will help. But we must ask Him for guidance. Not just once, but constantly. We must learn about those in office and those running for office. And then, we must make our voices known while being "in the world, but not of the world."

Merciful God, help me rise up and speak against the wrongs I witness. Keep me from apathy, but also give me the wisdom to know how to respond according to Your will. Through it all, keep me looking for Your Son's glorious return. In His name I pray. Amen.

Rock of Refuge

Be my rock of refuge, to which I can always go; give the command to save me, for you are my rock and my fortress (Psalm 71:3)

Scripture: Psalm 71:1-6
Song: "Rock of Ages"

Twenty-five years ago my husband and I loved hiking up a mountainside. Notice I said "hiking," not climbing. No paths. No ropes. No spiked shoes. Only sturdy walking shoes, strong legs, and healthy lungs enabled us to work our way upward. Tall Ponderosa pines sheltered us as we skirted huge boulders blocking our way and crossed icy streams on fallen logs.

God's peace accompanied us, broken by the joyful warble of a Townsend's Solitaire and an "Aha!" from my husband. He proudly held up an elk's antler—another one for his collection.

When we reached our "sitting rock," a huge, flat slab in a sunshine-filled space, we collapsed. Clean, fresh air and a light breeze revived us. "Look," I said and pointed west where snow-capped mountains towered, praising God in their majesty.

Holding hands, we prayed. "Thank You, God, for these moments of joy on one of your mountains." We picnicked, eating tuna sandwiches and an apple, and drinking cool water from a thermos.

These were precious moments of peace, a time to draw closer to our Creator. We needed only leave the noise and busyness of everyday life to find Him waiting. These memories bring pictures of God, my rock and my refuge, and I will praise Him forever.

Rock and refuge of my life, You are available at all times if I just open my heart to Your presence. I can find You if I just take the time to come to You. Thank You, in Jesus' name. Amen.